Bottom Dog Press
Literature of the Midwest
c/o Firelands College/ Huron, OH 44839

HUMAN ANATOMY
Three Fictions

Martin's World

A Well of Living Water

Moonless Place

Contemporary Midwest Writers Series #2
Bottom Dog Press

© copyright 1993
Bottom Dog Press
ISBN 0-933087-27-6
$9.95 First Edition

Cover art by Zita Sodeika
Edited by Larry Smith
Introduction by Laura Smith
Tyepset in Times Roman by Barbara Wrable

 The Ohio Arts Council helped fund this organization with state tax dollars to encourage economic growth, educational excellence and cultural enrichment for all Ohioans.

Introduction

The strategy for the novella or composite fiction writer is in combining short pieces, wholes in themselves, to fit a framework that somehow holds the collection as a solid work of fiction. Like life itself, composed of short, significant scenes in which one tries to perceive pattern and meaning, novellas allow for wide mobility in creating an overall theme that is, by the nature of the form, less directly pointed and, like a wide panorama, best viewed by standing back to encompass the contours.

This form of fiction arose from the Renaissance. Its roots lay in the tradition of oral narration where storytellers told a series of brief tales concerning the dilemmas and joys of human life. The tellers drew in listeners with drama and familiarity and wove tapestries of stories with a basic theme threading delicately through.

Staying true to the necessities of storytelling, novellas often captivate with realism. The collection here is strong in characterization, focusing on people's strategies for coping with the confusing pain of life, much like the themes of historical novellas. The unique aspect of this form of compiled short wholes is in providing completeness, like satisfying swallows, continuing until the glass is drunk. This form seems to be well-suited for real portrayals of lives and their episodic nature.

There are several strategies employable in creating a novella or composite fiction, and these differences in form are present in this collection. Philip F.

Introduction

O'Connor's *composite fiction*, *Martin's World*, derives its wholeness very loosely through the repetition of voice, settings, theme and motif, and a suggestive narrative line, as a certain tone or sense of life pervades all the pieces in the compilation. Annabel Thomas' *composite novella*, *A Well of Living Water*, maintains more consistency, including a narrative line, repeated characters, settings, themes and voices. Jack Matthews' work, *Moonless Place*, is the typical *novella* with a consistent narrative voice, setting, plot, theme and characters, yet it is more than a long short story or a short novel. The importance of maintaining the validity of a variety of fiction forms such as these is in opening to the writer more alternatives in which to pour creativity, affirming for the reader the right to choose lest we limit our world.

Unfortunately, this form and its variations have gone largely unpublished. Lost in the deluge of short stories that have become so prevalent and novels that remain a dominant form of popular literature, novellas have been cut or stretched to fit the mold. Novella writing has nearly become a lost art. Some remaining examples of successful composite fictions where the individual works echo each other and add up to more than a sum of their parts would include these classics: James Joyce's *Dubliners*, Sherwood Anderson's *Winesburg, Ohio*, Gertrude Stein's *3 Lives*, Katherine Anne Porter's *Pale Horse, Pale Rider*, William Faulkner's *The Unvanquished*, and John Updikes's *Beck: A Book*. *Human Anatomy: Three Fictions* attempts to revitalize the novella and composite form by presenting these three offered by major Ohio fiction writers.

The first piece is by Philip F. O'Connor, a San Francisco native who has taught at Ohio's Bowling Green State University, where he directed the school's creative writing program. "I have found a sense of order here that I did not have in San Francisco," he said of life in the Midwest where many of his stories and novels have been set.

O'Connor has created a style that "captures the life of people, the presence of places and the beauty of talk – so much so that we do not realize at once that we are in the very scene of our origins," remarked novelist Christopher Davis. This present work by this mature author continues his trademark of creative characterization through inner and outer dramas of personal pain and insight. This composite fiction is a carefully constructed portrait in which profound memories bubble to the surface and unravel a tormented history. The story unfolds from a deep point within a sharp perspective and is told in a simple yet profound voice.

The composite form helps this piece communicate like a dream. The colorful

Introduction

scenes climax and change abruptly, bursting through at different levels. The short sketches form a body of moving parts all stirring in one man who has unleashed a cutting wisdom without restraint, lashing out at a life that seems to be crumbling under his feet. The honesty in this portrait of Irish Catholic youth is stark and relentless. With nothing to lose, the man exposes his raw ghosts with biting urgency.

A Well of Living Water is written by Annabel Thomas, an author dedicated to the drive and strength of human character. She writes from Ashley, Ohio, compassionate celebrations of hard, earthy lives. Her presentation of complex emotions backed by clear characterization has earned Thomas a strong originality. She has been described as "embodying a viewpoint and vocabulary that are distinct and identifiable." Her accounts, told directly, haunt the reader like family legends of life and survival, colored with the character and diction of authentic lives.

Guided by the senses, her characters step through fear in textured journeys. *A Well of Living Water* pulls readers into the struggles of these people who face loss and tragedy heading into the wind with quiet fortitude. There always seems to be a small crack in the structure of sorrow that feeds enough light to keep them reaching toward warmth, toward each other. The glowing element that threads through the collection is a fire fueled by a grace beyond thought driving her people to move from the heart to create meaning in their lives.

Thomas' insight digs deep and renders accessible subtle emotions that sting in naked, honest familiarity. Life is taut and hard for these folks, so, with strong, calloused hands, they reach out.

Jack Matthews' novella *Moonless Place* is a character study of its professor narrator. It is written in his "deadpan charm" noted by Tom O'Brien in the *New York Times*. "He pretends to be innocent. He pretends to be sincere. He is not innocent and he is filled with guile," declares novelist Herbert Gold of Matthews. *Moonless Place* is a psychological mystery unraveling systems of introspection which the narrator reveals through examining the suicide death of one of his students. His innocence and sincerity is slashed through with cool, shrewd discontent.

From the lecture on Gothic literature that starts the story, Matthews, a professor at Ohio University himself, carries his readers into rooms haunted with faces and desires. "A belief in ghosts requires a second room," says the

Introduction

professor. "Thus, if there is another room contiguous to this one we are in, and there is a door between these two rooms ... the instant that door is closed, part of our imaginations is trapped in that other room." What is revealed in this novella remains hidden from its narrator. Trapped ghosts are at work in his rooms and they are fed by his disconnection from the people around him.

This variety of forms and themes presented in this book provides examples of new ways for the approach and execution of fiction. Deriving from the art of storytelling these variations of the novella form develop the idea of one tale adding on to and extending another to finally equal a whole greater than the sum. Another distinguishing feature of this particular collection is how the works mutually arise from the landscape of the Midwest, a land hearty in humanity contemplating under a wide and subtle sky.

                                            Laura Smith
                                            Portland, Oregon 1993

Martin's World

Philip F. O'Connor

©copyright 1993
Philip F. O'Connor
Martin's World
ISBN 0-933087-27-6

The author would like to acknowledge the following publications which first published these stories:

"The Man On the Bed" *Ball State Forum* VIII, 4 (1967)
"The Mattress" *Descant* X, 13 (1966)
"Story Hour" *four quarters* (1970)
"The Singer" *four quarters* (1965)
"Funeral" *Colorado State Review* (1968)
"Mr. Pizarro's Story" *Corona* 1 (1980)
"The Kissing Thread" *Seattle Review* III, 1 (1980)
"The Disciple" first appeared in *A Season of Natural Causes* (University of Illinois Press, 1975)

The Man on the Bed

The boy looks at the man on the bed. The man's gaunt face is pale yellow. His mouth is open and he is sucking in air noisily like old Uncle Dave drinks soup. His eyes are half-open but he seems to be looking at nothing. A bottle is suspended above his head. It is full of something like oil. An ominous rubber tube, burnt-red, extends from the bottle to the man's thin arm and enters it at the crook of the elbow. The tube is like a leash. The man is wearing a white shirt. It has no collar and no buttons down the front. His head is deep in the pillow. His body is flat against the mattress and a sheet is tight around it up to the chest. The man seems to be attached to the bed, a prisoner of the bed, of the sheet, or the tube.

The boy's eyes are wide with fright. His mouth hangs open, as though in imitation of the man's. Slowly, carefully, he reaches out and touches the man's arm just below the elbow. "Daddy?" It is a bare whisper.

The man continues methodically to suck in air. He does not respond.

The boy turns.

A young woman in white who has entered the room with him is standing just inside the door. She is staring at him. Her eyes are wet. She looks sick, like she is going to throw up.

"He didn't speak to me."

The woman says nothing for a few moments, then she raises her hand to her mouth and makes a whimpering sound like a puppy someone has kicked. She

Martin's World

turns and rushes out of the room. He guesses she has gone to throw up.

Now he is alone with the man. He stares at the man's face. Then he moves forward and presses his chest against the mattress. He leans toward the man, getting as close as he can.

The half-visible eyes seem to be trembling.

Again he whispers. "Daddy."

For a moment the sucking sound stops. The man makes an effort to turn his head toward the boy. Before the man's eyes meet the boy's, the head recoils and the sucking sound resumes, more noisily, like the noise a straw makes at the bottom of a glass.

"Daddy!" This time it is frantic. A plea.

There is no response. The man's eyes are closed.

An invisible hand reaches up inside the boy and pulls down hard, seeming to yank out his insides. He reels, loses his balance, then collapses to the floor.

Awakening, he feels the floor's coldness against his bare arms and legs. He wants to enter the floor's coldness. He wants to melt into it. But he rises and moves dizzily toward the door.

The boy is seated on an uncomfortable wooden bench with a high back at the end of the hall. He is looking at his mother. She is standing near the center of the hall. She is wearing her black coat. She is hunched forward, not facing him. There are several others. They all form a huddle like at a football game. One is his aunt. One is a priest. One is the young woman in the white dress. One he does not recognize. He is a tall man in a green shirt and green pants. The shirt is like the shirt of the man on the bed only it is looser. He has been talking a lot, moving his hands. The others have been listening. Now he puts one hand on the shoulder of the boy's mother. She nods. Then the man shakes the hand of the priest and starts toward the opposite end of the hall.

His mother turns to face the boy. Her eyes are very dark. The skin on her broad face hangs. Her mouth looks very big. Now her mouth opens. Though he cannot hear, he knows she is trying to speak to him. She seems afraid. It makes him afraid. He leaps off the bench and races to her, flying into her so hard he turns her half-way around. He clasps his arms around her thick legs and holds on tightly.

His eyes have been closed. Now he opens them to see the bench. There is no one between them and the bench. Still holding on he turns his head the other way. He can see the tall window at the opposite end of the hall. There is no one. The others have gone. They are all alone.

She pries him away. Then she takes one of his hands and holds it very tightly. He raises her hand and presses it against his cheek. They stand there for a very long time. It is like when they are standing in a big downtown department store while she tries to decide which way to go. In the department store he tugs at her coat, saying impatiently, "C'mon, c'mon." That always irritates her. She always says, "Leave me alone. I'm thinking." Now he does not want to tug, to irritate her.

Finally she releases his hand.

He looks up.

She is standing erect, staring at the door before them. She speaks but does not look at him. "Do you know what's happened?"

He doesn't, but he is sure she needs him to think he does. "Yes," he says.

"Let's go in then and see him."

The man's eyes are closed now. The bottle is gone. So is the tube. The man is not making noises any more. The boy pulls away from his mother and runs to the bed.

"Martin!" It is the voice she uses when he darts away from her on a crowded street.

He stops and turns.

"What are you doing?"

She looks at him for a few moments, then says, "Kneel down beside the bed." She looks angry but she sounds sad.

He obeys. He watches her kneel down beside him. She does not look at the man on the bed but presses her face against the side of the mattress and says, "Pray with me." Her voice quivers as she speaks the prayer. "Our...Father, who art in Heaven, hallowed by thy name..."

He does not pray. Instead he raises himself and peers over the top of the mattress. Impulsively he wants to climb onto the bed and pull at the man's long nose as he has often done in the morning to wake him up. He stretches toward the man. Again he whispers, "Daddy," this time sure the man will open his eyes and smile at him.

"Martin!"

He turns.

She has raised her head, is glaring at him. "Kneel."

He ignores her, turning, beginning to climb onto the bed. At the same time he reaches out, touching the man's arm. It feels very dry. The man does not stir. "C'mon, Daddy," he says, sure the man will awaken with a start.

He doesn't.

She is pulling at the back of his pants, saying, "Get down. Get down."

"No." He pulls away, grabs the man's arm and shakes it. "Wake *up*."

Martin's World

With a single fierce tug she pulls him to the floor, then spins him around so that he faces her. She sends her hand under his chin and snaps it upward. "Daddy is *dead*! Don't you know that?"

He pulls away and looks at the man on the bed. Still the man has not moved or spoken.

"Martin? Do you understand?"

"No!" he shouts. It's final, absolute.

The Mattress

The priest was the tallest man in the whole world. He had shiny hair and a heavy jaw and a long black cassock that swirled when he walked. His voice was like a baseball bat whacking an empty barrel. When Martin thought of God, he pictured Father Cyril.

"Bless me, Father, for I have sinned. It has been a week since my last confession. These are my sins: first, I took the name of the Lord, my God, in vain."

In the faint light of the priest's cubicle Martin saw Father wave aside his stole and bend toward the little screen separating them. "How many times?"

"Once, Father. No. Maybe it was twice." He knew there was a certain limit to the number of times one could commit a serious sin. Though he did not know what the limit was, he suspected that, when he reached it, the priest would erupt into an angry whirlwind and roar through the church, tearing down windows and doors and crushing the altar to marble dust. Such things had happened in his dreams.

"Well?" said Father impatiently.

He also knew that it was terrible to lie, most terrible to lie in confession. That was sacrilege. But he could truly not remember how many times he had blasphemed. It was not more than twice, so he said, "Twice, Father."

"Our Blessed Lord's name in vain twice," the priest said, shaking his head. "Such a grievous sin, and you have trouble remembering how many times you committed it?"

"I'm pretty sure it was twice, Father."

"And why did you take Our Lord's name in vain?"

It was late. There was no one else in the church. That's why, Martin supposed, the priest was taking time to penetrate. He tried to remember. It was difficult. He recalled only that the cursing had something to do with his nightmares. There had been two nightmares, nearly identical, but now he could only vaguely remember what they were about. He didn't want to have to think about them. He looked up and saw the priest frowning at him. "Something was chasing me," he said abruptly.

"Something was chasing you," Father said, as though he didn't believe him. "And what was chasing you?"

He thought and remembered but it made no sense. He said nothing, realizing how foolish he would seem.

The priest made a little growling sound and leaned back so that Martin could see only his hands. They were spread apart at the bottom and joined at the fingertips. The forefingers began to tap against each other, very methodically, tap tap, tap tap, tap tap, tap tap.

There wasn't the slightest stir of air in the tiny box. Martin's face was growing cold and wet and his body hot and wet. He twisted and turned, still looking at the priest's hands. Now the forefingers had stopped moving and were pointed upward, tensely. Finally he said it. "A mattress. It was a mattress, Father."

The priest descended toward him. His sour breath crept through the screen and bit at the boy, making his nose twitch. "What do you mean, a mattress?"

Rigid now, Martin closed his eyes. He did not want to go on thinking about the nightmare.

"Say what you mean."

Martin began to whimper.

"Stop that!"

"Mother," he said frantically.

"What about your mother?"

Frightened, he had thought of his mother and had uttered her name. He wanted her to come and take him out of the confessional and hold him until he was no longer afraid.

"What about your mother?" the priest repeated.

Perspiration stung his eyes, making him close them.

"You cursed at her. Is that it?"

"No!" He began to cry.

"Stop that!"

He bit his tongue, forcing himself to stop. He gripped the sides of the little ledge on which his elbows had rested. Opening his eyes he saw the priest's hands again. One of them moved forward into a narrow shaft of light. A watch appeared, flickered, then vanished. The hand with the watch then shot upward. Martin did not wait to see that it moved only to the priest's face, where Father began rubbing the stubble on his chin. The boy jerked his head back, sure the hand was coming through the wall to strike him. In a way it did come through, invisible, slicing like a knife at the curtain that had separated him from his nightmare and tearing open the knot that had tightened around his vocal chords. His words poured out. "It was so big ... and it came closer and kept getting bigger and bigger. I tried to get away ... but I couldn't. And then I ... and then I ... and then I ..."

"Stop!"

Martin beat his fists against the soft asbestos wall above the screen and shouted, "It kept coming! I tried to kick it! Again! Again! I hit it! It wouldn't stop! Wouldn't! Wouldn't!" He stopped with a strangled cough and fell back softly to his heels, panting, exhausted.

The priest pressed his puzzled searching face against the screen. "What's the meaning of this?" he said.

Martin lay groaning. He did not hear the priest.

"Answer me!"

Dizzily the boy pulled himself up, trying to remember where he was.

"Did you hear me?"

Martin looked up and recognized the priest.

"Confess that last sin and confess it calmly!"

Martin said nothing.

"Damn it! Confess!"

It sounded like the horn of a distant train, rising and rising in volume as it came closer. He pressed the palms of his hands against his ears and opened his mouth, as though to release some of the invading sound. He began to roll helplessly from side to side. One shoulder bumped lightly against the wall; the other touched the curtain. Back and forth he went. When his shoulder hit the curtain for the third time, a splash of light entered the box. It startled him. He put up his hands, as though to protect himself from something, and lost his balance. He fell sideways, past the curtain and into the aisle.

He looked up to see the priest standing over him, seeming to rise to the church's ceiling. "Get up!" he commanded.

At first Martin thought Father was lifting him. But it wasn't the priest. He was rising all by himself. At the same time he was swinging his fists frantically. "I'm sorry," he said, but as he spoke he saw himself hammering the priest's legs. "I'm sorry," he repeated, and he ran from the church.

He stared at the yellowish scum on top of a stagnant pool in a little creek near his home. He extended his foot gingerly, and with the sole of his shoe he scraped away some of the scum. For a long time he gazed into the dark muddy water.

It was a round white mass, soft and very big, bigger than the house, bigger even than the church. It *was* like a mattress. A gigantic rolled up mattress. A gigantic rolled up mattress. And it was floating toward him where he lay. He started to stand up to face it, but his legs wouldn't work. It was moving faster now, very fast. It came over him, darkening the sky. As it descended, he beat at it with his fists, but they were tiny and helpless against it. It pressed down on him, and he could no longer move. He shouted at it. "Stop! Please stop!" No use. In a moment it completely covered him. He could feel its suffocating softness against his face. Overcome simultaneously by terror and rage, he cursed, violently, helplessly.

Awake, he raced through the dark hall to his mother's room. He threw himself across her bed, reaching out until he touched her.

She wasn't asleep. "What were you shouting about?"

He scrambled onto the bed and pressed himself against her. He said only one word. "Nightmare."

She took his hand. "All over now," she said. "We'll talk about it in the morning."

In the morning he awakened to see her standing over the bed, dressed, gazing down at him expressionless. She was rocking the bed with her knee. "What was the nightmare about?"

"I don't remember." He didn't.

"Sometimes God sends nightmares."

"I know." He turned away.

"Look at me."

He obeyed. Her eyes were black pinpoints. They seemed to be fixed not on him but on something beyond and beneath him. "The other night you shouted in your sleep. Then last night again. What were you dreaming about?"

"I told you, Mother. I don't remember."

She continued to stare.

"Please, Mother." He wanted her to look at him.

She did not seem to hear. "Someday you'll want to leave me."

She had said that at other times. He did not know why. "I love you!"

She clicked her tongue against the roof of her mouth. "You say you do."
"It's true," he said desperately. He reached out, trying to touch her.

He tried to swing toward her, but his feet were caught in the blankets, and he could barely move. "Please," he said, reaching out again.

She waited, watching him struggle, then came down over him. She pressed against the bed with her open hands. It tipped under her heavy weight.

Her face seemed to expand enormously as it approached. He closed his eyes and felt her cold cheek touch his. He felt her wet lips on his ear, then on his cheek, then on his mouth. "I'm afraid that someday you'll want to," she said. There were tears in her voice.

"No," he protested. He wrapped his arms around her neck and held her tightly. When he opened his eyes, he saw one of the tiny faded red flowers on the aging wall paper. "Never," he said.

"No, " she said, returning his hug, "don't. Not ever."

Now he plucked a young weeping willow branch from the tree beside the pool. With it, scraped away more scum. He could see his reflection, distorted, in the ripples. It frightened him. Still holding the willow branch, he turned and ran for home.

He stood in the kitchen doorway, studying her.

She was at the stove, holding a long wooden spoon, stirring something in a large pot. At first she did not see him. When she did, she turned, seeming frightened. "How long have you been there?"

"Just a minute or two."

"You're all flushed. Have you been running?"

He nodded.

She put the wooden spoon on the stove and, wiping her hands on her apron, came toward him. "What on earth for?" She led him to the table. She poured a glass of milk and brought it to him.

"It's not true," he said.

"What's not true?"

"I wouldn't do it."

She pulled her hand away. "Wouldn't do what?" she said suspiciously.

"Curse at you."

"Curse at me? Who said you had?"

"Father Cyril."

"Father Cyril? Why would Father say a thing like that?"

He was looking at the table. "I guess he got you mixed up with my nightmare."

Martin's World

"Your nightmare?" She had begun to back away, toward the stove.

"It came back to me at confession."

The pot had begun to boil over. She turned, picked up the spoon and began to stir.

He raised his eyes and tilted his head, as though something important had occurred to him. Then he rose and moved slowly backward toward the door, still holding the willow branch at his side.

She did not see him. Stirring and talking she said, "You must have been thinking bad things about me. You must have cursed me behind my back. Why else would Father say what he did? I've been afraid of you turning on me, and now you have." She went on talking, not aware that he had hurried, as though driven, through the hall.

He stood before her bed and glared at the clean white spread. Then he raised the willow branch above his head and began to beat the spread. Again and again he beat it, until the branch seemed to harden his hand. Finally he screamed—It was a joyous scream!—and rent the air with a terrible curse.

Story Hour

"Sit quietly. Sit quietly and behave yourselves." The nun, the frowning nun who was old, had been telling them about God and wars. "I won't say it again. Sit quietly now."

Martin had no knowledge of wars but God was with him always. God was the holly bush at the back of the priests' house. God was the sweetness of the holly berry if one could taste the holly berry. Martin was looking now at the holly bush at the back of the priests' house, between the priests' house and the priests' garage. How gleaming were its leaves, and the berries bristled red like drops of blood.

"And Jesus said, 'You shall be soldiers unto My Father.'"

Martin was seven-and-a-half, nearly eight, and sometimes he cried in the school yard when the sun went away, cried and ran home, afraid his mother had not returned safely from work. Sometimes, not always. He was good at basketball and the other boys liked him, but they looked at him like a stranger when he cried.

"...and Jesus is with our boys who are fighting. They write me, some of them I've taught, and they tell me how much they need Jesus, and they know Jesus is with them. The ones who were faithful to him in school are the ones who write the happiest letters." Her hands went up and she spoke between them to the ceiling and she said, "God have mercy on our boys. God have mercy."

In the priests' garage there was a car, a long green car, and the priest with a voice like the man who gave the news on the radio, he owned that car, it was his own car. And the priest, when he crossed the school yard and saw Martin put one in the basket, clapped his hands loudly and said, "Keep shooting, boy." Always the same. "Keep shooting."

The school yard was a large black square except where it was painted white for basketball, and Martin played after school until it was time for his mother to be home from work or until he cried. Sometimes the bigger boys' elbows pumped down on his mouth or ear and he had to go to the side and hold himself where it stung, but he didn't cry, not for that he didn't.

"It is for us they're fighting and some of them will give their lives like Jesus. When you stop to think of it, how beautiful it is. Have any of you here ever thought what a sacrifice it is to give up your life for someone else? As Jesus did? As our boys are doing? Have you?"

One by one hands went up until many hands were up. Martin didn't put up his hand and neither did three or four of the girls, but all of the other boys put up their hands.

She said, "Martin, I'm surprised."

He said nothing. He rarely spoke.

She said, "Quite surprised."

He smiled at her and shook his head, apologizing, and then he looked out the window.

There was smoke coming out of the garage now. He could not see the big roll-down door for he was facing the side of the garage but was sure the door was open because he could see the smoke. It was bluish smoke from the car of the priest who looked like a boy. That priest had a car smaller than the green car and not as beautiful.

"What are you looking at, Martin?"

She caught him by surprise, for he thought she was no longer looking. But he told her the truth. He told her he was looking at the smoke.

When he said "smoke" all the children looked. It was a cold day and the smoke held together and went white as it rose, going to puffs turning to streamers, brilliant white and was very pretty. Martin had looked to see the smoke and then the green car when it came out of the garage and the priest in the green car. Now everyone was looking.

The nun had been speaking hard but now she spoke softly and said, "Martin, are you waiting for Father Devlin to appear? Is that it?"

Again he told the truth, by nodding, nothing more.

She said, "I should reprimand you for not paying attention." She smiled and all her teeth, which are large teeth, seemed to show. She said, "But I won't. I think I understand." She looked about. She said, "It seems a lot of boys have made Father Devlin their favorite. Is that true?"

Martin turned to see all of the boys' hands go up along with his own. He glanced back to see if the green car had started into the broad driveway, where it would go around the holly bush and then out to the street; it hadn't. He turned to the nun, not wanting her to speak to him again about looking at the smoke.

"Do any of you know what Father Devlin did before coming to St. Francis'?"

A boy's hand went up at the back. The boy was David and had a very deep voice and was taller than Martin or anyone else in the class. He had taught Martin how to shoot a basket over his shoulder. He said, "Wasn't he a chaplain?"

"That's very right," said the nun. "He was indeed a chaplain. He was a chaplain with our troops." She waited and looked down at them, looked back and forth across the classroom at all the faces, and when her eyes landed on Martin he smiled into them. "A chaplain," she said, "and he saw many men die." Again she waited and again she looked. There had been many little noises from the children fidgeting and rolling pencils and playing with ink wells, but after she mentioned the priest having been a chaplain and seeing men dying there weren't any noises.

She said, "Father was near the battlefield and said Mass every morning, and some of the men he said mass for didn't come back in the afternoon, and that hurt him terribly but it was his reward to know they had heard God and partaken of the Holy Sacrifice before making their own final and supreme sacrifices. Oh, if only he would, the stories Father could tell you."

She surveyed the faces again. There wasn't even a twitch. All were waiting for more. She smiled at them waiting. She smiled and fixed her glasses on her long nose and closed her eyes and raised her head and seemed to be thinking and when she lowered it she said, "Does anyone know why Father left the war and joined us?"

She waited and waited as though having a contest to see if someone would guess or maybe sneeze or drop a pencil or do something that might trigger an answer, but no one did, and so she said it: "He was wounded." It was a whisper but a heavy whisper all of them could hear. "He went into battle to be with the boys and one day he was wounded."

There was a low appreciative moan. One boy uttered, "Gee!" It was almost "Geeze!" The nun had warned them not to say "Geeze." "Geeze" was short for "Jesus" and it was blasphemy. Martin watched the boy who said it and the

Martin's World

boy was grinning embarrassed the way someone grins when he almost does something wrong but catches himself. Martin bent down and grinned with the boy, in sympathy with the boy, but the nun did not ask him what he had said, did not make sure it was all right. She was more interested in telling them about the priest and the war.

Martin did want to hear more about the priest and how he was wounded. He wanted more than ever to see the priest. He thought of taking a chance and turning once more, to look at the smoke, but he didn't.

"He was given a medal by the general," she said slowly, and after pausing she added, "The officers and boys in his brigade took up a collection for him after he was wounded." Again she paused. "When he got back to this country, he found something waiting for him, a gift from those he had served." Once more a pause, and then: "Martin, can you guess what the soldiers gave him in appreciation for what he had done for them and their dead comrades?"

Martin gazed up at her. Why had she asked him? He did not know why and did not find out for the answer to her question had begun to throb through him and when he recognized it all else seemed quite clear and he knew it was only right that she ask him, inevitable, as was the answer itself: "A ...a car. They gave him a car."

"Exactly! How bright of you, Martin!"

The other children turned in admiration but he didn't see them for he was stunned, almost stunned, by his own answer which was pristine and like a needle piercing everything, the spotless blue sky and the face of the nun and the smoke, the pretty smoke outside.

"He came back wounded and found the car waiting for him. He had done so much! And in appreciation the bishop gave him his choice of whatever parish he wanted and he chose ours. How fortunate we are! How very fortunate!"

Most of the students nodded but Martin did not nod for he was no longer listening. He had felt himself shooting up the immense needle to the very top of the universe where he imagined himself, in total darkness, holding on. It was magnificent, and frightening!

"What did you say, David?"

Martin had remained at the top of the needle and had heard David's voice and it had alerted him and he had listened. Now the nun's words were flying up to him through the darkness. Martin listened. It seemed terribly important that he hear, as if David's question or the answer to it might be his only release from the needle.

"Where was he wounded, Sister?"

Martin opened his eyes, waited.

The nun looked down from the platform on which her desk rested and she looked at the tall boy David and she didn't speak for a few moments and when she did she spoke hesitantly. "It wasn't the same kind of wound you think of. ..when you think of soldiers being wounded. It was...." She looked at her hands on the desk. She looked at the children. "It was a wound all right, a real wound, but. . . ." She raised her hands and opened them before her face as she sometimes did, to slap them together over a hovering fly, only now she didn't slap them together. She gazed between them, "How can I say it?" She remained still, as though the world had suddenly gone to ice and caught her where she was. She was silent and motionless for a long time. When finally words issued from her broad mouth they came in a strange haunted basso like the muted beats of a dirge. "It was...it was a wound. It was a terrible wound...." Her hands came down slowly and her face went, twisting, into pain.

All eyes held her, waiting, as if they, the eyes themselves, knew she wasn't finished.

She looked at them, the children's eyes, then knew, or seemed to know: "I ...I can't tell you." It was a naked whisper: "I can't explain."

She went from religion to arithmetic very quickly, ignoring small grumbles from several of the boys.

It was at the end of the arithmetic lesson that David stood and shouted: "Look!"

Martin turned and saw David standing and pointing out the window, his finger shaking.

Martin looked. The smoke was gone. The boyish priest was kicking wildly and he kicked again and again and then he reached down and tugged at something and Martin knew it was the handle near the bottom but the door didn't open and the breeze flapped through his cassock and he rose up and hammered at the door but it didn't open and then a fat woman Martin recognized as the priests' housekeeper came out of the house and she was wearing an apron with flowers on it and the young priest spoke to her and she reached down and helped him pull at the door but still it didn't open. In the distance Martin could hear them calling, "Father! Father!"

"Close the blinds!" The nun had stood and was waving her arms and shouting, shouting first at David in the back and then at all of them. "Close the blinds!"

Nobody moved.

She came swishing off her platform and stumbled to the first blind and grabbed the string and pulled hard. "Close them in back! Close them this minute!"

Martin's World

No one moved.

She leaped to the second blind and yanked it down. "Close them!" she screamed.

No one seemed to hear.

"You don't understand!" She banged her leg on the radiator going for the third, the blind opposite Martin, and she groaned but went on and got the string and pulled and the blind flew down with a ripping sound, stayed.

But Martin had seen. He had seen the young priest take the handle, had seen him pull against it with his life, had seen the door burst open, had seen the priest and the woman surrounded by a mountain of smoke.

She stumbled on but did not reach the back window in time. David shouted. David said, "They're carrying him out!"

"Stop it, David!"

David said, "They're pulling him on the ground and his coat is up! I can see his shirt and his stomach is sticking out! They're pulling him toward the holly bush!"

"David!"

"They've gone past the holly bush!"

She reached up and her hand snapped at the string of David's blind and she brought it down, slashing down, and she turned on David and spoke fiercely to him through teeth that were yellow and tight: "Be silent, you *cur!*" She stood before him and glared at him until he sat down. She raised her eyes. "Be silent! All of you!"

And they were.

The Singer

Godless mobs of delinquents roamed the beach on Sundays. That's what his mother said. Still Martin turned left instead of right at the street corner, out of sight of the living-room window. He felt tight. It was his heavily starched shirt and tweed suit. The suit was too small for him now.

Last First Friday he'd shouted and then fainted during Mass at the parish church. He woke up in the hospital emergency room and saw his mother crying. Two doctors were speaking to her. He saw her turn her head and say, "Why?" One of the doctors answered her, but Martin couldn't hear. Then that doctor came to Martin and said, "Come upstairs with me and tell me what happened."

Upstairs Martin said, "It was Communion time and I was saying my prayers getting ready when the whole church went white like lightning came into it, and I thought that's what it was until Jesus started wiggling on the cross to get off. I thought He was climbing down to get me. I shouted at Him not to hurt me. But He didn't hear me. I remember shouting. Then I forget."

The doctor looked at him for a long time. He didn't seem angry, but why wouldn't he say something?

"You don't believe me, I bet. Once I saw St. Joseph move his arm and smile down at me. I was seven or eight. I was at the Communion rail. He was holding this lily with a long stem. He pushed it toward me and smiled like he was telling me I had nothing to worry about. That's the only other time. It happened, though.

Martin's World

I'm sure. Do you believe me?"

The doctor seemed to be trying to hypnotize him. Staring. Smiling.

He began to get angry. He didn't know why.

Finally the doctor said, "Why do you think you fainted?"

"I didn't faint," the boy said. "There was a light. I think the Holy Ghost came into the church."

"Do you believe that?"

"My mother goes to Mass and Holy Communion every morning before she goes to work, and benediction every Friday night. Sometimes on Sundays she goes to three Masses before I even wake up. She visits the sick about once a week and goes all the time to pray for dead people at funeral parlors, even though she doesn't know who it is."

"How old are you?"

"Nine. Do you believe anything I say?"

The doctor nodded.

"Everything?"

"No."

The boy turned his thoughts to himself now. He wondered why he was asking the questions he was asking. He was beginning to like the doctor. "My mother is waiting."

The doctor said, "Stay." Both of his hands rested on the top of his desk. He looked at one of them.

It would be better if the doctor were angry. "My mother makes me go to Mass and Communion every Sunday. If you have faith, you don't need anything else. That's what she says." She hadn't said it, but she might have.

"Do you like going to church?"

Martin hesitated. He nearly said he didn't. He'd been missing Mass lately on Sundays. But he didn't say that. What he said was, "I don't really mind except for wearing my best shirt and pants. They're tight. I want to wear loose clothes, but my mother makes me wear these."

"*Makes?*"

"She wants me to."

"You said *makes*."

"I didn't mean that. She never forces me to do anything. It would hurt her feelings if I didn't."

The doctor waited, studying him.

The boy felt very uneasy now. "I'm leaving." He stood. He expected the doctor to protest. When he didn't, Martin said, "What happened in church is none of your business, you know."

The doctor didn't seem to hear him. He said, "I think you should come back and see me once in a while."

"I don't think my mother wants me to."

"Do you care to ask her?"

"No."

"Then I will." The doctor stood and led the boy to the door.

He noticed the same boy every Sunday. He had dark skin and a deep jaw and wild and shiny wavy hair. He always seemed to be at the center of the group. The others Martin didn't remember Sunday to Sunday, but this boy he remembered. He was tall and barefoot and wore slim faded white pants and no shirt and seemed to be speaking constantly. To the sky and to the sea. The others listened. Sometimes he would break from the group and run and plunge into the sea and the others would cheer. He nearly told his mother about the wild boy one Sunday but didn't when he realized that telling her would let her know he hadn't been to church.

"I won't be around to look after you all the days of your life, and that's why it's good I put you on your own now and let you go to Mass by yourself."

"What would happen if I didn't go?"

"What makes you say such a thing?" Her eyebrows fell into a frown. "Don't ask such questions."

"I mean if I weren't me, but someone who didn't like to go to church."

"God has his own ways of punishing. It's not for you to ask."

"Did you ever miss Mass?"

"Never," she said firmly. "Never deliberately."

"I wonder what would happen. Pagans don't go to church."

"Pagans pay for it. Pagans aren't happy."

"Some of them must be."

"Some of them must be?" she repeated. "Name one. Name a pagan who's happy."

"I only know Catholics."

"A good thing. At least you have someone to turn to. Who has a pagan to turn to? No one but himself. And that's the one person he needs to get away from."

"Maybe a friend. Maybe he could turn to a friend."

"Friends don't have the answer. Only one person has the answer. That's God."

"I wish God would let himself be seen once in a while."

"You're denying your Faith when you say a thing like that. What kind of Faith is it that has to have God around to reinforce it?"

"Just once in a while. If he would maybe appear in the sky once in a while."

"And wouldn't that make things awfully easy for us?"

"Did you ever wonder if He wasn't in the Holy Communion wafer?"

"What's coming over you?"

He didn't know. He lay in bed for a long time that night wondering about it, but still he didn't know. Tomorrow was First Friday. If you attended Mass and received Holy Communion for nine consecutive First Fridays, you wouldn't die in mortal sin and be condemned to Hell. Tomorrow would be his ninth. If he made it to Holy Communion he would never have to worry about dying with the sin of missing Sunday Mass on his soul. A priest would find him first. He would confess.

"Did you get to Communion?"

"No," he said removing his tie from his pants pocket. Someone had taken it off and put it there.

"God help us? What does all this mean? You were minutes away from insuring your salvation and then something happened."

"I couldn't help it. It just came over me." He put his tie on the kitchen table. "The doctor said I fainted."

"Well, did you?"

"I don't know."

"We'll have to pray extra hard tonight. Maybe it's not meant that you should make the nine First Fridays."

"Why would it not be meant?"

"How do I know?" She removed a loaf of bread from the paper bag full of rolls and bread she had taken from the bakery where they had stopped on the way home from the hospital. She'd told the bakery owner she wouldn't be able to work for the rest of the day. Her son had gotten sick at school. She handed Martin two slices. "Put these in the toaster. A little toast will do you good."

"What could it mean?"

"What could what mean?"

"God not wanting me to make the nine First Fridays."

"I told you I don't know."

"Do you think I should talk to that doctor again ... about what happened?"

"Of course I don't."

20

She poured herself a cup of tea and took it to the kitchen window where she peered out at the rolling gray mass of fog that was sweeping in over the house. "Jesus, Mary, and Joseph ..."

"Mother."

"... give us succor in this time of great peril."

It was the voice he often heard when he used to go with her to seven o'clock Mass. A strange droning voice. Deep, distant, and soft. Not meant for his ears. It had always frightened him. As though while she was lost in her prayers, something might happen to him and she would not know it. He was frightened now. He spoke to her again, but she didn't hear. She never heard him when she was praying.

"... and if it be your will not to give the boy a chance to insure his salvation, at least then give me a sign as to why you are doing this. Let me know what has gone wrong. Is it something he's done? Or thought? Dear Mary and Joseph. Patrons of families. Intercede with your Divine Son so that I may know ..."

He felt suddenly envious of the invisible young boy Jesus to whom her prayers were directed. He'd felt envious at other times. But now it was worse. He nearly burst out and shouted, "I hate him! I hate him!" He didn't shout. He was afraid to.

"Eat your toast," she said.

Once the dark boy picked up a smaller boy and ran with him to the surf. The boy who was being carried didn't cry out. In fact he was laughing with the others in the group who were watching. Martin wondered why the small boy was not afraid. The dark boy held him high, then hurled him into a rising breaker. The small boy was still laughing when he stood and struggled to get back to the beach.

"I know," she said one day after they'd finished saying the evening rosary together. "It came to me while we were praying." Her tone was solemn but sympathetic.

"Why?" he said eagerly.

"It's those questions you've been asking. I suspected as much, but wasn't sure until now. He gave you a sign." Her eyes met his. "You must give yourself unquestioningly. It's the price of salvation."

Martin was relieved. He'd been afraid God had told her he'd been missing Mass on Sundays. That night before falling asleep, he promised himself that he'd stop asking question. It wouldn't be hard to stop asking. Not as hard as it would have been to stop going to the beach.

Martin's World

Each Sunday Martin crept closer. One Sunday he had sat on a piece of driftwood waiting for the group to pass near him. He was going to say hello. He was going to look the dark boy right in the eye and say hello. But the group was late that Sunday, and he didn't get the chance. Just after they appeared—specks on the distant beach—he turned and looked up the hill to the church. The congregation had begun to pour out onto the street. It was time for him to go home.

"What did the priest have to say in his sermon this morning?"

"I wasn't listening very closely," he said.

"You haven't listened very closely for a long time. What's the matter with you?"

He punctured the soft orange belly of the egg before him. "Nothing," he said.

"At least you're not asking foolish questions anymore. That's a good sign anyway."

He felt malicious. He didn't know why. "What did the doctor tell you?" he said.

"What doctor?"

"The one I talked to."

"He's not a real doctor. He's a psychiatrist." Her hissing told him she was getting angry. "What's someone like that doing at a Catholic hospital anyway?"

"He was nice to me."

"That's part of his game."

"I don't think he wants you to force me to go to church."

"Force you? What makes you say that?"

"I don't know. I just had that feeling."

"It doesn't surprise me. Kneel down."

He did so.

"Our Father, who art in Heaven, hallowed be thy name. They kingdom come, thy will be done. On earth, as it is in Heaven . . . "

"Mother?"

She had knelt beside him. "Pray with me. Give us this day –"

"Stop!"

"Pray."

He did. "Give us this day our daily bread and forgive us our trespasses as we forgive those who trespass against us. And lead us not into temptation. But deliver us from evil. Amen."

"Go to your room now."

He went to his room. He tried to pray alone, silently. The voice he heard was his mother's, not his.

It was a beautiful day. Very bright and not too hot. He slipped on his swimming trunks before putting on his suit pants. He went to the kitchen to kiss her goodbye.

"You pay attention today now."

He didn't reply.

On the way to the beach he thought of the doctor. He wished the doctor were with him. Maybe the doctor would be out walking and would see him.

When he reached the dunes, he scanned the beach until he located the specks. He rushed stumbling across the dunes, tearing his tie from his throat and his shirt from his back. At the piece of driftwood, he undid his pants and let them fall to the sand.

They were close enough to notice him. He waved. Someone pointed to him. A girl. The dark boy stopped. That meant everyone stopped. There were about a dozen of them in all. They were wearing loose fluttering shirts and blouses. And shorts. And swimming trunks. The dark boy was wearing his same slim faded white pants. His skin seemed darker than ever today. He put his hands on his hips and looked at Martin.

"Why are you stopping?" Martin whispered.

The dark boy seemed magically to have heard him. He cocked his head. He began to walk toward Martin. The others followed.

Martin's heart swelled, pushing against his ribs. It was hard for him to breathe. "Hurry!" His legs quaked. He held the piece of driftwood for support.

Some of the others rushed ahead of the dark boy and swarmed around Martin.

He didn't notice them. His eyes were fixed on the dark boy.

The dark boy came closer and smiled.

Martin broke the pieces of driftwood and rushed toward him. He could see nothing but the dark boy's smiling eyes. He ran as fast as he could. At the last moment he thrust out his hands. Too late. He crashed into the dark boy's middle.

The dark boy fell back. "Hey!" Then he reached forward and plucked Martin off his feet.

"The surf!" someone yelled. And he yelled it too. "The surf!"

The dark boy raised him above his head and spun him around and around until he began to feel dizzy. His trunks were coming loose. He held them with one hand. The dark boy spun him faster and faster. Martin couldn't see. Finally the dark boy shouted, "Now!"

The icy shock made him scream. He tried to stand. He fell. Cold salt shot into his nostrils. He tasted it. He couldn't breathe. He leaped up but fell again. He tried

Martin's World

to raise himself with his hands. A breaker hit him from the side. He rolled over. Now he couldn't feel the bottom. Now he could. He stood on his toes finally and turned in a circle. He saw the breaker which had hit him but he couldn't see beyond it. On his tip toes he pushed himself toward the beach.

Heads appeared above the dying breaker. The dark boy's was the highest. The dark boy was laughing. "What's your name?" he called.

"Martin!" He trudged through the backwash until he reached the dark boy.

"You're a damn fool," the dark boy said.

"I don't care." He looked at the others. They were all smiling at him.

He glanced toward the pieces of driftwood. He saw his suit pants. Beyond that lay his shirt. Above that the church. People were beginning to appear on the steps. Soon there would be more of them.

The dark boy and his followers had started down the beach. The dark boy began to sing. What a strange voice, distant and lonely like the wind. Not wanting it to fade to silence, and stop, Martin hurried after it.

The Disciple

My mother and my step-father never kissed and he was a scrawny man and she a big woman, big as a mountain, and they never kissed and rarely spoke and I sat between them and listened to their forks click-clacking and waited down the years for them to say something, God knows what, waited and waited but nothing was ever said, I give you my word, unless you want to count the fights when he shouted *Fishwoman!* and she screamed *Cur!* and he kicked doors and she threw herself on the sofa and I ran from one prison of a room to another until I found my bed and lay down and swallowed it all through my ears and thought myself a saint.

He was a white old man, round and soft like my mother and there was dandruff on his wild eyebrows and cassock shoulders. I always sat right beside him at the desk in the chaplain's office and sometimes he put his hand on my shoulder when I spoke. His breath smelled like fresh milk boiling.
So you want to be a priest, Martin.
Yes I do, Father, very much.
And why do you, Martin?
To help the world, Father.
That's noble, Martin, that's noble. A Jesuit like me?
No, Father, I'd rather be a parish priest working with families.
It's a fine calling just the same. There's more than one way to serve God.

The student who was closest to a friend got a car and we went to the movies together on Friday nights and then he asked two girls from his neighborhood and they came with us and we went to the drive-in and I sat in back and held Marjorie's hand until one night he told us he'd brought something to put in the Cokes. The girls giggled and looked at each other and went to the rest room and came back and said, *All right, Arthur, you can put it in.* He got the Cokes and put it in and then even the screen credits became funny and all the cars shrunk and I laughed and they looked at me. Marjorie's dress was up and I sent my hand to her thigh and she yelled but I squeezed and didn't let go and Arthur said *Stop!* so I did. Then Marjorie cried and threw up.

And why don't you think you're good enough for the priesthood, Martin?
It's some of the things I've been doing, Father. With, with girls.
Girls? Many girls?
One, Father. And it was only once.
That doesn't seem so bad now, does it?
I, I didn't seem to be thinking, Father, I touched her in, in an impure place.
His arm circled my back and he drew me toward him. *The sins of the flesh are the hardest to resist.*
Yes, Father.
At night, Martin, are you troubled by impure thoughts?
Yes, Father, often.
He lowered his head so that his ear nearly touched my shoulder. *Satan works every minute of the day,* he whispered. *Pray, Martin. Pray before you climb into bed and pray to the Blessed Virgin. She will give you strength. When you lie down think of Mary and her Divine Son, think of the suffering they went through for you and for me, Martin, for mankind. When your thoughts are driven down into darkness, think of them.*

We prayed together and afterward he brought me toward him, held me, terribly tightly, said, *You're a lovely boy, Martin, and you'll make a lovely priest.*

When I left he was weeping. Hunched forward, his face in his hands, weeping.

Angelo was still working when I got to the margarine plant after school. It was his job to open the vats and get them ready for me to clean. Angelo always waited beside the vegetable oil vat and told me about himself. Angelo was married. Angelo didn't have any kids. He had a cord in his penis tied so he wouldn't have kids. He had other women. He stayed in the city after work and drank beer and had other women. He took them to a little hotel room if he had money. He took them down under the freeway when he didn't. He stood them up against a pillar under the freeway and did it. He was about thirty and had slit eyes and when he smiled his mouth didn't open. He was very thin and dark and he had almost a woman's face. While he spoke he scraped off hardened pieces of vegetable oil from inside the tank and rubbed them together in his hands.

What do you think of that, eh?
What does your wife say?
Hah! I don't tell her.
Doesn't she mind your drinking?
Hah! I'm the boss.
How old are these ladies?
Some old, some young. I go by looks.
Do you, I mean, have a tough time, I mean getting them to, I mean?
Listen. They like it more than men. More! Didn't you know that?
No.
They do. Sometimes I could have three, four women. Women are hungry.
You mean the ones you know.
All women. Show me a woman and I'll show you someone I can screw.
Not all women are that way.
Every woman.
Bull, Angelo. I was thinking of my mother.

He stamped his foot. He hit the side of the tank with the flat of his hand. He shouted: *Every woman!*

Angelo was a liar.

I stood by a woman in a side seat on a streetcar and her knee rubbed mine and I leaned away but her knee followed and I looked down and she was pretty with a hard face and I closed my eyes and stood there wanting and not wanting her and her knee moved up between my legs and I imagined it coming all the way up and touching me, stone against stone, and I couldn't breathe. I ran for the exit and down a strange street. I thought she was thumping after me, so sure I could even hear her breathing. I ran until I found my home and then I looked back. She wasn't there and the moment I knew she wasn't there I knew I wanted her.

Father, how would I know if I didn't have a real vocation?

Martin's World

Ah, Martin, that's a matter between you and God. There's no one can tell you but God.
Through my thoughts?
Oh, deeper than that, Martin. It's in here he tells you. He raised his hand, opening it, and slapped it against his chest. *Through the soul.*
It's something you feel then?
Yes, partly that. He folded his hands over his paunch and leaned back in his chair and slowly raised his head and closed his eyes. *A beautiful feeling.*
Yes, Father.
Very beautiful.
Father?
He opened his eyes and smiled at me down his face. Yes, Martin?
I don't think I have that feeling.

He closed his eyes again. His face had a placid look, like the look on the fixed face of someone in a coffin. He seemed, in fact, to be dead, peacefully dead, or at least in a very deep and happy sleep. He was smiling, still smiling, smiling certainly. *You do, though, Martin,* he said. *Your eyes are on God.*
But, Father...
Your eyes are on God and though you be tempted night and a day they will remain on him.
Father?
The eyes of a boy driven by sin or dark downcast eyes, crusted with lust, the eyes of an... the eyes of an animal. I have seen them, Martin. He leaned forward seeming to descend, and his own eyes, round and slightly protruding, opened very wide now, in a stare, fixed on mine. He seemed suddenly terrified, or a little mad. *The eyes tell everything.*

I waited.

He shook his head and said in a businessman's practical way, *Oh, none of us in the priesthood can deny having had our doubts. None of us. But in the end we submitted to the will of God and allowed it to direct us.*
I'm not sure I know how to do that, Father.

He took my hands in his and looked at them. *Say to Jesus,* he whispered, *my will is thine and thine mine. Say that.*
Now, Father?
Yes, now.
My.
My will is thine.
My will is thine.
And thine mine.

And thine mine.

He raised my hands and pressed them to his lips. *Martin,* he said hoarsely. *Oh Martin.* I needed my step-father then, surely it was then I asked him to come with me to the school football game and then that he said it depended on his breathing and then that my mother said, *Go with him can't you?* and then that he took his coffee and went to the darkness of the living room and sat in his big chair by the radio and turned it on and laid back and tilted his head and, wheezing, gazed down at the base of the curtain as though searching for a lost speck of something, sat there and sat there until the night came and hammered itself into the roof and never gave me an answer. Then he died.

My mother will probably need me to stay home and work after I graduate, Father, so I don't think I'll be going to the seminary after all. God will find a way. Speak to him. He will find a way.

I went to church every morning and took communion and asked God to do a lot of things, none of which I remember very well, and then just to do anything, clear the air, whatever he wanted. Make me want to or not want to go to the seminary, make me know or not know that my father had loved me, make the sadness go out of my mother's eyes or not go out. It was up to him.

My mother took a job running an elevator in a department store and began to drag herself about the house like someone with a wooden leg. Her skin sagged and lost its color and her eyes went under her eyebrows and she spoke in grunts and said rosaries and dropped dishes and coughed and said, *Martin, what on earth are we going to do?* I fled to school in the morning and to my room at night and said, *I don't know, Mother. I don't know.* She soared to the sofa and wept as though I were my father.

Come on, Angelo said, *I got a tiny one just for you.*
I've got to get home. My mother isn't well.
She's forty-two but likes young guys.
She looks so bad she might have to go the hospital.
She's five-by-five but like a jumping bean in bed. I guarantee.
She's dying!
She's jumping!
No!
Yes!

I locked my ears and took my mother for walks in Golden Gate Park on Sundays and we bought stale bread and fed the ducks like she said we used to do when I was little. We found abandoned paths and trudged over them, heads down, wearily searching, as though for precious stones. She always grew tired and had to rest on a rock or stump. I stood by her, silent, and then took her arm and led her home.

Arthur said where have you been keeping yourself and I said around I guess and he said I got another car a convertible and am going with this great blonde from Abraham Lincoln and every weekend we go up to her folks' place on the Indian River it's a ball I'm telling you they don't even ask for I.D.'s in the bars and we use the swimming pool at this big resort and you're invited anytime Marty she said bring your friends.

It sounds great, Arthur.
It really is. I'm not kidding.
I wish I could go but I can't. It's hard to explain.

I pictured Arthur's girl and she was golden born out of the sun and I imagined having her naked on my bed and in the back of Arthur's car and on a beach that was like a great white quilt and she loved me more than Arthur and we never told him. It was more fun that way. Poor Arthur.

It's nice you're going to be a priest, Martin.
I've changed my mind, Mother.
Your father would have been happy.

She talked about Father Waters up at the parish rectory and how he took his mother for rides on his day off and how the two of them walked arm in arm when they went shopping on Saturdays and how there could be no greater reward for a mother, no matter what the sacrifice, and,

Don't count on it, Mother.
I might buy myself a little car and go see you on visiting Sundays.
But.
Pack a picnic lunch and the two of us sit on the lawn beside the chapel and.
No.
You'll write to me, won't you, Martin? You'll write every day.

I said, *You have to listen, Father. I can't be a priest. I'm sure now I can't. I don't feel it in me.* I said, *Lately, I've been troubled more than ever by impure thoughts.* I said, *I've been fighting them off sometimes, but they're getting worse and make me think I'll never get rid of them all the way.* I said, *How could I be a priest and hear confessions and stand up in a pulpit and tell people what to do if I was always trying to get rid of desires, terrible desires, Father, and I have them every time I look at a girl on the street.* I said, *Father, please listen to me and try to understand. I admire you so much and all the other priests so much and I wish I was a better person but I can't. Father, I just can't.* He must have nodded a hundred times as I spoke, rocking back and forth in his chair, his eyes leaping whenever I paused, signaling me to go on, do go on, saying yes yes yes, why haven't you had the courage to tell me this before now.

But when I finished he continued to rock and his eyes continued to leap every few seconds, as though all the time he had been listening to someone else, someone saying things he wanted to hear, another boy, a sacred clean boy of his mind.

Finally all of his motion stopped. He was staring at the framed picture of Jesus across the room. Lost to me.

Father?

He did not reply.

Father?

Nothing.

I rose, backed toward the door, left the office. I don't think he saw me.

I almost said yes to Arthur but couldn't because of the scene I kept picturing, me at a brightly lit cocktail lounge with a loud band at the back and lots of people, all gazing with me at a dark corner where an enormous woman in black was bent over a tiny chair and retching until a stream of something poured whitely from her mouth and filled the air with platinum light.

She went to the doctor and the doctor said the cardiogram showed she had probably had an attack in recent months or maybe years for her blood was not getting to where it ought to at the right speed or rate and if she wanted to live more than a few years she would have to take it very easy, very, very easy. No job and only light housework at best.

I went to church and told Jesus I knew he'd done it because I wouldn't be

Martin's World

the boy she wanted and said I was sorry but promised to work hard to keep up the house. I looked at his aching face and told him I deserved everything, said if it meant I would have to feed her with a spoon or carry her to bed I would do it. I stared at him for a long time, as though he might reply.

Once I saw the chaplain approaching in the hall and was about to say good morning when his eyes, which had momentarily found mine, reached sideways, found those of another boy, stayed on them until he had taken the boy's sleeve, caught his attention. As I passed them he was saying, *Jerry, Jerry, Jerry where have you been? I haven't seen you all week.* He sounded very happy.

Angelo said, *C'mon.*
I said, *No.*
He said, *C'mon.*
I said, *No.*
Angelo said, *C'mon.*
I went.

She smelled like the disinfectant in a men's room and took me to her place in an old hotel and came down on me like a lid and called me *Love* and said *Give give give give give!*
I gave nothing. I grabbed my pants and rattled down the noisy stairs and into the city past ranting cars and tinny bars and alleys that were black and voiceless and stumbled and fell into a filthy gutter and bumped my head and came up choking and saw a million specks, brilliant and flooding my eyes. God had sent the universe off like a rocket.

She was face up on the sofa with one immense leg, bare and blue-streaked, over the side. I sat down beside her and rubbed her back.
It's a hard life, isn't it, Martin?
Yes, Mother, it is.

Funeral

When he was a young man in college he had this idea: he would write a story of his own funeral. The teacher said, "You can't do that. How can you write about what you haven't seen?"

He didn't write the story.

They were winding up the hill with his mahogany box and he saw them in his dreams but not only in his dreams. They put the box in a hole. His mother was there.

He worked in the city after his classes, downtown in the city, and there was a man with no legs who sat on a coaster selling pencils. The man's clothes were dirty and he had one eye.

"Do you ever have thoughts you're afraid to share?"

"Not often," his friend said.

Somewhere he read that Sartre, though afraid, felt freer in Nazi-occupied Paris than he had anywhere else. Sartre said every move he made had significance. Sartre said he knew then what freedom was.

He told that to a teacher.

The teacher said, "Well, that makes sense."

Martin's World

Someone banged the coffin against the side of the grave and it tipped and fell and everyone heard it crack but no one suggested raising it up again and repairing the box. Not even his mother.

"I've hardly seen a funeral, maybe one or two, but I dream about my own all the time," he told his friend.

The friend said, "You can't take such things too seriously."

He said, "Do you ever dream such things?"

The friend said, "No."

There was this girl who lived next door when he was a child and her father beat her often and she went into the back yard and cried but when she came out to the street to play she was never crying. She did well in school and was now a chemical technician, living at home still.

"It's amazing the things you see that aren't in books," he told his friend.

His friend agreed.

His friend became an accountant after graduation. He himself drove a truck. He would drive the truck until he could decide what to do.

"You should make yourself some money," his friend said.

"I'm not very ambitious."

"And meet people. Who can you meet driving a truck?"

"No one really."

He lived by the sea. The ships came in, the ships went out. When the work was light he drove to the park near the bay. The water was mysterious and so were the ships, especially the ones going out. He watched them for hours. Where were they going?

A leg came out of the coffin, naked, white, wiggling. There was no sound. Just the leg.

The truck was an old truck and went slowly up hills. The city had many hills. There was something between him and the truck, a kind of trust. You could leave the truck in gear on some hills. On others you had to put on the brake. He got to know the truck and the hills where the truck would stay and the hills where it would not. There was no reward for knowing the truck and the hills. The man who owned the business died. His son sold the business and the truck.

He sought another job, on trucks. There was something about being able to think and speculate and wonder while sitting behind a wheel. Trucks were the best for him. He would drive another truck. A big truck on the highways.

One employer said, "Experience is important if you want to drive one of those rigs. You haven't enough experience."

Another said, "Are you in the union?"

He wasn't.

He took up, finally, with a drug store, driving a small truck for a chain of drug stores. The driving was constant.

In the evenings he went to the library to find books on the mind that dealt with questions he couldn't answer by himself. It was hard for him to find the books he wanted. Once in a while a phrase suggested something: "We live the dreams of ancestors as well as of ourselves." But really, very little.

A man reached in and plucked off the leg. They marched down the hill and put it in a fire. After the fire they put the ashes in a wheel barrow and took them up the hill. They sprinkled them on top of the dirty coffin. They filled in the hole. The mother hadn't cried but when the dirt was on the coffin her knees buckled and she cried. They pounded the dirt with their feet. They sprinkled seed on the dirt. They put up no headstone. The grass grew. You could not tell someone was buried there.

He got deliveries done early one day and had some time for the bay. He was sitting on the strip of sand by the water when two girls came by. They were high school girls. They sat not far from him. They did not look at him. He threw little stones into the water where it lapped. He listened:

"He's so kooky."

"I know, I know. Geraldine dated him and said he took his shoes off at the movie."

"No!"

"Honest to God!"

"Then he wanted to take her for chili dogs out near the beach. You know, at the amusement park."

"That filthy place?"

"She said she wouldn't go. He took her home and asked her to go fishing with him the next day."

"Fishing?"

"She said she had a surfing date with Eddie."

"Oh god!" Laughter. "Fishing!"

"Imagine!"

He was lying down now and his arms were over his head, flat against the sand and his face was in the sand and he tasted the salty taste of the sand and clip-clapping of the little waves went on and went on and he listened and tasted the salt taste of the sand and fell asleep.

When he got up he was cold. He took his truck back and was reprimanded for being late. He understood the reprimand. As he headed for the streetcar he saw a manhole cover pulled partly away from its hole. Had he not been looking he might have missed it and fallen in, all the way or partly in. But he saw it and avoided it.

Mr. Pizarro's Story

Mr. Pizarro didn't come to meetings very often and when he did he didn't speak.

Anna said Mr. Pizarro why don't you come to meetings more often.

He didn't answer.

Anna said why don't you answer me.

Mr. Pizarro looked out the window.

He had a harelip and starey eyes and his hair was full of silver. He was older than Anna and the rest of us. He never smiled. Someone said he once had a business of his own. Someone said his wife ran away with the manager of the business. No one knew. He stayed in his room a lot and slept.

One day when he stayed in his room someone asked Anna why do you ask Mr. Pizarro so many questions.

Anna said we all speak. Mr. Pizarro should speak. Who is he not to speak.

Maybe he doesn't want to speak someone said.

I don't want to speak sometimes said Anna. But it's good to speak. We have to speak to get well.

We turned to the doctor. Why doesn't Mr. Pizarro speak someone said. Why does he sleep so much.

Only Mr. Pizarro can tell us said the doctor.

Martin's World

Then Jimmy came. He didn't speak either but he was trying to. He stood up and pointed at old Mrs. Williams and said *nnn...nnn...nnn*. He sounded funny but no one laughed. We knew how hard he was trying.

When Mr. Pizarro came again Jimmy sat next to him and looked at him a lot. Then he made a noise.

Look at Jimmy Mr. Pizarro Anna said. Look and see how hard he is trying. Mr. Pizarro looked.

He likes you Mr. Pizarro but you don't help him. If you spoke maybe he would say something. Why don't you speak to him Mr. Pizarro.

Mr. Pizarro kept looking at Jimmy but he didn't speak.

You don't help anybody even yourself Mr. Pizarro.

Mr. Pizarro turned to Anna and made a spitting noise but he didn't spit.

The next day Mr. Pizarro didn't come to the meeting. Jimmy walked around with his eyes wide open like a blind man. We were afraid. He touched some of us. He touched Mrs. Williams' face. Mrs. Williams giggled. Someone said you shouldn't giggle Mrs. Williams. He's trying to learn. Mrs. Williams giggled anyway. Jimmy wrapped his arms around her and pressed himself against her. She laughed and said *Ooo* like she was being tickled and the loose fat on her arms wiggled.

After the meeting some of us asked the doctor why did Jimmy go to Mrs. Williams.

Why do you think he said.

Someone said maybe he doesn't like Mrs. Williams.

The little girl Jessie said maybe he wanted to play with Mrs. Williams.

Anna said no I think Jimmy thinks Mrs. Williams is his mother. The doctor looked at Anna and said I think you are right Anna but only Jimmy can say for sure.

The next day Jimmy walked across the room and knelt down in front of Mrs. Williams and pointed at her stomach. Mrs. Williams did not giggle. She put her hands over her stomach. Jimmy tried to pull them away. He spoke for the first time. He said please.

Mrs. Williams did not let him pull her hands away.

Then Jimmy fell to the floor and cried.

Mrs. Williams was frightened. All day she walked around holding her stomach.

Jimmy did not stand up or speak again until Mr. Pizarro came to another meeting. He walked around and stopped in front of Mr. Pizarro. Mr. Pizarro didn't say anything. Jimmy moved closer. There was silence in the room. Mr. Pizarro didn't budge. For a long time Jimmy stood there looking down at Mr. Pizarro and Mr. Pizarro looked up at him and kept looking until Jimmy made a noise. Then Mr. Pizarro looked out the window.

Anna said say something to Jimmy Mr. Pizarro.

Mr. Pizarro kept looking out the window.

Jimmy made a noise no one understood.

Mr. Pizarro didn't seem to hear.

What are you looking at Mr. Pizarro said Anna.

Mr. Pizarro didn't answer.

Say something to him Anna shouted.

Mr. Pizarro stood up and walked out of the room.

Anna went to Jimmy and stood beside him and held his hand. I hate Mr. Pizarro she said to the rest of us. I am almost well but I hate Mr. Pizarro.

The next day no one came to the meeting on time. When everyone finally sat down the little girl Jessie started crying.

What are you crying for someone said.

After a while Jessie said I am crying because of what Anna said to Mr. Pizarro.

Why should that make you cry said Anna. I just wanted him to help Jimmy.

I don't know said Jessie. She kept crying.

It is Jimmy we must think about now said Anna.

Jimmy did not walk around or try to talk until Mr. Pizarro came again. That morning he went to the center of the room. His face was not shaved. He was in his pajamas and was not wearing his bathrobe.

Where's your bathrobe someone said.

Jimmy did not answer. He was looking at Mr. Pizarro.

Mr. Pizarro looked at Jimmy. This time he looked at him mean.

Mrs. Williams giggled.

Shut up Mrs. Williams someone said. Jimmy wants to say something to Mr. Pizarro.

But Jimmy did not say something. He started bouncing slowly up and down on his toes. He seemed to be smiling.

He is acting like a little boy someone said.

Why are you doing that Jimmy.
Why is he doing it doctor.
The doctor said Jimmy will have to tell us.
But he won't talk.
Then we won't know said the doctor.
Talk to him Mr. Pizarro.
Mr. Pizarro only watched.
Jimmy was bouncing very fast now. While he was bouncing his penis fell out of the opening in his pajamas.
Jimmy! said Anna.
The little girl Jessie put her hands to her face and turned to the back of the chair.
Mr. Pizarro stood up.
He pointed. Look he said.
Jimmy looked at Mr. Pizarro's eyes. Then he looked down Mr. Pizarro's arm to his finger. Then he looked at it.
Button up button up said Mr. Pizarro.
Jimmy's hands moved to cover it.
Button.
Jimmy looked at Mr. Pizarro's eyes.
He can't someone said. How can he when he can't even dress himself.
Button.
Jimmy looked down. Then he looked at Mr. Pizarro's eyes again.
Mr. Pizarro was still pointing. Now his finger was shaking. Button.
Jimmy looked down again. Then he pulled the flaps of his pajamas forward and covered himself. Then slowly he began to button his pajamas. Mr. Pizarro smiled. It was the first time we had seen Mr. Pizarro smile.

Mr. Pizarro came to other meetings. When Jimmy stood up and remembered things Mr. Pizarro looked up at him. When Jimmy started to forget Mr. Pizarro said don't stop now. Then Jimmy would squint and try hard to remember.
Once Jimmy called Mr. Pizarro Father.
Mr. Pizarro twisted his harelip mouth and said I'm not your father.
Anna said maybe you should be his father for a while.
Mr. Pizarro shrugged.
That afternoon he went swimming for the first time. He took Jimmy. It was Jimmy's first time too.

Pretty soon Jimmy did not need Mr. Pizarro. He was shaving all by himself and dressing by himself. He made a little boat. He played chess with Clarence the social worker. He helped people. Like the little girl Jessie. He took Jessie for walks in the rose garden.

One day Anna said to Mr. Pizarro you helped make Jimmy better. I'm sorry I shouted at you.

Mr. Pizarro shrugged it was nothing.

When are you going to tell us your story someone said.

I don't have a story said Mr. Pizarro.

You wouldn't be here if you didn't have a story.

Mr. Pizarro shook his head. Again Mr. Pizarro began to sleep a lot and he didn't come out of his room even for the meetings. They had to bring his meals to his room on trays. Sometimes he wouldn't eat when they woke him. Then they would have to put the food in his veins through a needle.

Jimmy went to his room with Anna one day and said please come to the meetings Rudy.

You must said Anna. I won't ask you to tell your story anymore.

Anna and Jimmy waited but Mr. Pizarro did not answer. He lay on his back facing the ceiling. Then he turned on his side and faced the wall.

They watched him and still they waited.

Finally Jimmy said will you come Rudy.

Mr. Pizarro spoke. He said no.

Martin's World

The Kissing Threads

He asked me did I have a brother and for a minute I didn't remember and he said I think you had a brother and then I remembered. I remembered we were laughing but I knew that couldn't be right because there was blood in his face, coming out of his eyes.

"Tell me something about him."

The doctor has an oval head that reminds me of a grape and the first time I thought about that I laughed out loud. He said why are you laughing and I didn't tell him. He said are you remembering something funny and I said no. He said something must be making you laugh. I said yes but I didn't tell him.

"Did you two play together often?"

We had a bucket and a big stone and Mr. Bevilockway gave us a rope and said don't hang anyone. My mother wasn't home. My father was dead then. I was older than my brother. He did not make fun of anything I did or how I looked. We were going to make an elevator in the tree because we had seen Tarzan do it in a movie. I made him get in the bucket because I was so big. He got in and then I threw the rope over and climbed up on a branch, the one we had climbed up to with the ladder to put the rock on a branch.

She said they had a Pekingese dog when I was born and he used to come in and try to bite me in the crib and they had to give him away. And when my brother was born she said I acted like the Pekingese dog. I hit him and pinched him when he was in her arms. Don't you see how you frighten him, she said. But all I remember is loving him even when I was mad at him.

"Are you listening, Mr. Donovan?"

I said no and he nodded like he was understanding I wasn't listening but I was or couldn't have answered and I laughed and told him that and he said ah ha like he knew I was really listening and even understood why. He laughed and said did I want to tell him why I was laughing and I thought of something funny to say but I didn't say it. I thought of saying why are you laughing at me laughing if you don't know why I'm laughing.

We went up to Red Hill sometimes and we were always laughing up there because of the cardboard boxes that were flat and we found them where the big boys hid them and slid down the front of the hill and then put them other places. Not where the big boys had left them, and that's what made us laugh, and even more when we went back once and one big boy kept looking under some bushes for his box and saying my sister came here and took it, that's just what she'd do. We were way back behind a Eucalyptus tree and we laughed so much without making any noise we wet our pants.

There was a weeping willow tree in the lot but we made the elevator in the apple tree in our yard and I remember him sitting in there with his arms around his knees tucked in and the rock was sharp on the sides sitting on the branch where we put it. I got the other end of the rope and climbed up to the branch.

"Do you remember asking *me* if *I* had a brother?"

I asked him that the last time because of his mouth. I almost wanted to cry. His mouth was hanging down when he was sitting there waiting for me to say something and it made me think of my brother's when I used to hold up something, like a stick, and say I'm going to hit you. But if I saw his mouth I just started to shake seeing how afraid he was and then the doctor's mouth went down like it was going to get ugly crying in a minute so I asked him something. I asked him if he had a brother. It was one of the first times I talked to him.

My brother was afraid in the bucket too because I remember his voice saying, will I go up fast, Martin, but I didn't care if he would, it was like, now I think or maybe then I thought, it was like I was born just born to make him afraid. Will I go up, Martin, and hurt myself? I said no and don't be a baby. I think he wanted to cry then but he knew I would make fun of him and I put my leg around the branch and tied the rope around.

I said to the doctor, "Now we can stop."

He said, "We have been here for only a few minutes." He said, "You are

Martin's World

speaking. You have been speaking." He said, "I am proud of you, Martin."

I wanted to cry then and I want to now but I am not and I just think because I am writing it down like I won't know what happened even though it did happen just a little while ago, until I write it down. I am holding back my crying until I write it down. If someone came in my room now I would kick at him until they went out until I wrote it down because I don't know yet or something. I am just writing it down, wanting to write it down.

Sometimes I see boys playing in the park across from the hospital and I know they are brothers, not because of the way they look, the shapes of them or anything, but the way they move even if they aren't close together like there is some way one turns, maybe the little one, after the big one stands or something and I think inside there are things working that tell one when the other is doing something and he moves and there is something between them like music. Once we went to this movie about two brothers and they had been Siamese twins or something and when one got hurt even though they were far apart the other one felt it and we both said, I remember in bed we both said, it was the best movie we had ever seen.

"Martin?"

Now I am sorry he told me to write things down. I have to put what is in my mind on the paper but I don't want to. I think I was crying when he said Martin. I am crying now, remembering what I was thinking about then. He wants me to talk when I cry or feel bad. That's when I don't want to talk.

I didn't want to hurt my brother. When we got home from the hill once he said what would you do if those big boys came over and put a rope on our hands and tied us up in a tree and I said I would get away but I was afraid after he asked me that, not afraid they would tie us both up but would take him away from me and high up on the hill someplace knowing that would be the worst, knowing it from looking in my face and taking him up and laughing and throwing stones down at me when I tried to follow and get him back. I was afraid of that.

"Do you want to talk about it?"

"No!"

I got up. He said, "Sit down, Mr. Donovan." But I had to walk around. I was feeling very fast, seeing the walls turn around me and my arms went hard and I got them together, my wrist touching my other wrist, wanting to walk around and just look at my hands to keep my head still. I think I said Michael's name.

"Sit down."

He looked up with his mouth spread wide like it was broken and the blood in his face, his eyes were very wide, it covered his whole face and his mouth was grinning through it and his eyes searched up the tree to see me. Then the blood was in his eyes. He fell on the dirt.

"It slipped!"

"What, Mr. Donovan?"

Mr. Bevilockway said, you probably killed your brother.

I got up and shouted something. I don't remember what.

He got off his chair and was saying my name.

I was swinging at Mr. Bevilockway, not him, just wanting to have the hate go through my arms and legs but he was pulling me from behind back into the chair and I saw my arms and legs moving.

"Calm down, Mr. Donovan."

They took him in Mr. Bevilockway's car and I said I want my brother, I want to go with him, and they locked the door of the car. Some other man waited under the pear tree outside the window after that and when I opened the window he stood down there looking at me. My mother was with him and Mrs. Bevilockway, looking up, standing behind the man like they were there to help him if I tried to get out through the window. Get him! I kept shouting at them. Find him! If he was dying if he was hurt why weren't they with him. Why didn't they get him, why didn't they let me see him.

I see my brother in his bandage even though he's dead. His eyes look out of the two holes and I put my arm on his back when we walk someplace and I am afraid someone will push him or hurt him and he'll bleed through the bandages and this time he'll really die even though he's already dead. I touch him and he says, that's all right, Martin, like I didn't have to touch him and I say to him I love you so much Michael and want to go with you all the time and just stay with you and everything and keep saying that and touching him and where it hurts on his head. I wait until he's asleep in our bed and I feel in the dark where the threads are and bend down and kiss all along the threads like I'm making his head get well.

I don't want to hurt him. I love him so much. I love him so much now. I want to say that. I love you so much, Michael. It is the only thing I have to say.

Martin's World

Clock Time

I can now admit to a truth I may never be able to speak again: I am weary and dry on this black December night and cold with the cold of old men long gone from all but the motions, patterns, gestures of the moment. My thoughts no longer wind around the possibility of actually being there, grappling with, trying to make something of...

I appear before students at designated times in designated places and usually begin by asking a question. I've assigned a play. Yesterday I told them to examine the character of the protagonist. Today, appropriately, I ask my question:

"What do you make of his hesitations?"

His what? the nearest set of eyes say.

The question is suddenly followed by a thought: *Somewhere men are dying.* It makes no sense. There are wars and I think of a current one in Latin America but thinking about it makes no sense, no more sense than my question. Far less sense than the answer given by the student I have pointed to.

"Nothing." He apologizes with a shrug.

"And you?" I point to another whose hand is upraised.

Are they freshmen or sophomores? I can't remember. It is not important.

"He was too indecisive." The reply comes in high-pitched cocksure tones. "That was part of his personality."

Martin's World

I am sick. I think I would say, "Yes, go on." But I am sick at the sight of the scrubbed and eager face of him who has just spoken. I turn away from it. I look at the gray face of an unkempt young woman at the back of the room. I want her to answer. But she never speaks. I turn back. The eager student wants to say more. I do not say go on. I do not even nod. I wait. One, two, three seconds? I feel them staring at me. Finally the unkempt student looks up. It seems to be a signal for me to speak. I say to them all, "Go home and reread the play. Let's try to make more of it next time." I do not say it cheerfully or angrily. I just say it.

The words of the eager student hammer at me as I flee down the dimly lit hall, flee so as not to give one of them the chance to catch up and say something he or she thinks significant.

Was that the morning or early afternoon section? I don't remember. I don't try to figure it out. It seems important not to try to figure it out.

I see in his gray denim jacket the only member of the department I can, for no clear reason, bear. He always smiles, but he lives with terrors. Someone is going to take away his favorite courses. He won't get a contract next year. Whether or not he does, he will spend the summer trying to make approvable a dissertation he started some years ago. "There are factions working against me," he said.

"Coffee?"

I nod.

"Out of class early, eh?"

"I didn't feel like torturing myself or them for a whole hour."

He smiles at that. He once said he likes me because I often reveal my feelings. "I have to," I told him. "It's that or another term in the bin." He laughed. He never reveals his feelings. But I know them. I read them in his face. I hear them in his voice. As clearly as if he spoke them out every day.

"I'm using Bradley next hour," he says.

"Bradley is good," I say. "Bradley knows what the play is about."

"I'm going to read to them."

I nod. "That way you don't contaminate Bradley."

We cross the street to the coffee shop. There are tufts of snow on the student union lawn. The sky is lead-heavy and darkening. Is this the morning or afternoon coffee? I don't know. Not knowing pleases me. I have a secret: I am living on the edge of a mystery, on the verge of a discovery. Day or night? Up or down? Here or not here? Yes or no? History's contradictions seemed captured in my uncertainty. It's all topsy-turvy. I begin to feel almost giddy. I don't want an answer. If a solution must come, I want it to come slowly. Let the mystery last.

We are at the door of the student union. He says, "Where were you at eleven-thirty?"

"Eleven-thirty."

"I went to your office to see where you were planning to eat lunch."

I shake my head and mutter, "Damn."

He does not know why I said "damn," yet he laughs. Unusual responses make him laugh.

We enter the faculty lounge. Today, for some reason, there is free coffee. If this is afternoon, I missed the first section. In each I have one student who is to come to my office if I have not appeared and tell me there is class. If I am not in my office, the student is to use my phone and call my apartment and then return to class and tell the others to wait a few minutes, I'll be there. Today a student called the apartment, and I went and taught, rather began to.

We sit with our coffees. There is a lot of noise rising from the tables. He says where shall we sit and I say why ask me and he says is something bothering you and I say you and he says me and I say something you said and he says what and I say it's not important and he reddens and so I end by saying, "It's trivial and funny, and someday I'll tell you about it, and we'll both laugh."

I hold my coffee cup and watch other faculty. There are several of them, some from engineering, some from science, now us. They are talking fast and excitedly and, it seems, simultaneously. What are they talking about? I hear "hockey" several times. The college has a good hockey team. There may be a game tonight. I have never been to a hockey game. Once I had an interest in baseball. *Sports are for the young*, I think, and then I think, quite unexpectedly, *When will it happen?* It has no meaning. It vibrates through my mind like the dull note of a bass violin. *When will what happen?*

They are talking about lots of things and the coffee has made my mind work faster and I begin to listen and hear and I learn that the semester is to be shortened because the students want to get started early on summer jobs and that some government department has given a team from our physics department a new research grant that will allow it to study drinking water in large cities and that there are rumors that the board of trustees is planning to get rid of the president because of his inordinate personal spending. There is more. Those who aren't speaking sit coiled, ready to join in. Those who are speaking smile as they speak, and they seem to be arguing but they aren't, only speaking rapidly—ratta-tat-tat, tat-tat— and a little frantically. They are either speaking or waiting to speak.

I feel a chill. My friend or I has left the door open. I am about to get up and close it when I think, *Why close it?* So I don't. I just get up and leave.

I hurry through the dark passageway, where a warm breeze swirls about me, then up the stairs and out onto the sidewalk. Students approach and break around me. I hurry to the back entrance of the humanities building. Inside the hall is warm and dimly lit. The stairs are narrow and painted black. As I hurry upward, the heat envelopes me and I begin to perspire. My office is off a little hall behind the stage of the auditorium. Someone has turned off the light and the hall is dark. I feel for my key, then for the lock, then for the door handle, which I turn. The office is too dark. I close the door, feel my way to the venetian blind, pull a cord and open the blades slightly, move around my desk to my chair, and sit down. I still don't know what time it is, only that it is afternoon.

Eventually I notice a procession of car headlights descending along the highway of a nearby mountain. The mountain is the last of a range that separates the town from the lower, more populated, part of the state. The highway skirts the town and passes northward into Canada.

It comes again: *When will it happen?*

Later, sometime later, the firehouse siren will shriek. For me it will be the signal that night has finally established itself, having come down over the engineering building and the science building and the arts building and the stores and the houses and the streets and the lawn, over all the night descending.

And Then And Then And Then

Evidence:
The eye is the hand of a worm. The worm itself is a hand.
This.
More.
Bearings. What of bearings?

Well, I am here, sitting a few feet from that window. Save the sky, nothing is visible but the naked branches of a surviving elm. I cannot see the building behind the wall next to the window.

But the worm is an eye traveling around the wall next to the window, moving, freely freeing me.

In summer, driving with my uncle, I said, *I can close my eyes and say I don't know who I am or what I am. When I open them I don't know.*

That, he said, *is fanciful and can be injurious.*

My own child, of another time, would have said, *why?*
I did not.

What do you think you'll do when you're older? he said.

I did not have an answer. It was a question I had never considered.

We live in a flat and ugly town. No one is happy here. Or everyone who has spoken to me about it said, *I am not happy here.* That or equivalent.

I have thought, *This is purgatory.*
It is not.
The travel of the worm may be purgatorial travel.
Are there boundaries in spiritual places?
When was Shakespeare in Denmark?
In the *Concise Cambridge History of English Literature,* the editor of the Shakespeare section speaks of his plays:

> They contain elementary mistakes of fact. They are unoriginal in substance. They are haphazard in form. They are full of loose ends. They are thoroughly untidy. They contain singularly few literary allusions. They bear every mark of hasty improvisation. They smell of the theater, never of the study. They are not, in any respect, considered works. (p. 257)

London was a gray Babylon. What could he see?
The worm is an eye, leaping outward.
Inward.
Darling, I ride the eye of the worm sliding into darkness.
I am alone, she said.
I am here, I said.
Go away, she said.
I am here. You must understand.
Your being, not your acts, betrays you.
I will speak of my being as act. I have never been able to ask a woman to let me touch her. Yet I have touched and been touched. I have no rights in that regard. I become an actor at times, especially when drinking. I say something like, Let's get a room together. Once in a while one of them softens and leans toward me. But there was only that one—oh, I hate the word—affair. I am not forgiven. Should not be, I suppose.
You deserve her.
The point...
It's too late. It was too late before we started.
I have no other woman. It's only that I hesitate to ...to touch you. That might be the difference. Please touch me.
Not again. Ever.
The sky, an uneven gray, moves slowly past the tree, whose trunk and branches remind me of the illustration for the human nervous system I saw in the

Martin's World

children's encyclopedia, though there it was scarlet and here it is black.
　We were walking. Alexander said, *How far do the stars go up?*
　I said, *All the way.*
　He said, *To where?*
　I said, *To the other side of the universe.*
　He said, *What is a universe?*
I did not say, the distance a worm, as eye or hand, can travel.
　We are all stumbling. For some it is a game.
　It is not a game.
　The eye of a worm has traveled around the wall next to the window.
This time it finds no building.
　I write:
　　　This morning a large building disappeared from the campus. Students
　　　and faculty bound for classes there noticed the loss. Nothing has been
　　　reported in the paper. In the building's place were mounds of grass and
　　　a few tall trees. It was one of three science buildings. Classes scheduled
　　　there have been moved . . .

I write no more of that.
　But I am writing.
　The reality is in these words. Those too. But now these.
　It is your responsibility, she said. Get the book done. I have to have freedom. Something in me must be released. It's fine for you, thinking you see what you see and writing it down. Wonderful! Where's my therapy? I too must be free.
　You are wrong about nothing.
　Then?
　I don't know how to answer you. I answered another question today. I answered it for the boy from the student newspaper. He said, Tell me your favorite contemporary writers. *I once would have named two. But that would have been because I'd not seen how far they've not dared to come. Do you know, the first now bores me. I like them both, at least compared to others, but . . .*
　I'm leaving.
　For a walk or for good?
　For good.
　And I will now declare that the universe is the distance I, my worm, the eye of my hand, travel.

A good life conquers many things, my uncle said.

Dad? Alexander said.

The fiction of the plains, on which we now live, is a fiction of closed metaphors. Sherwood Anderson's hands, eggs, fences, trees. Nothing is terribly distant. What is good is lucid. Like the movements of a worm the rhythms of prose are limited by the surfaces on which it travels. But the eye of the worm is always open.

I am here but not here, Uncle.

Not the sky but words are the limit.

Dad?

What?

How far?

So far that it comes back the other way. Up up up up up up up up, but all the time coming back. If you were a worm that could stretch as far up as you wanted, up up up up up, you would eventually come back to the place you started. Do you understand that?

Yes.

I said to her later, *Do you understand that?*

No.

Writer One, you have not worked out the kinship between words and things as they are or, if you will, appear to be. You have gone farther than most of us, but you have not made, passionately made, the connection. It is my severest criticism of you, my only one.

The tree. The tree must stay. The story will be no better or no worse for the movement of the tree. The tree will stay.

The phone rings.

I answer.

It is Alexander. *I like the new lady,* he says. *She told us there is a giant frog in our attic and if we don't do what she says it will swallow us.* He laughs. *What are you doing?*

I am wondering what happened to the building that used to be next to this building. Remember? Where that science-stuff is we looked in the window at?

Is it gone?

Yes.

You mean none of it is there?

None of it.

Gaoww! Did someone blow it up?

I didn't hear an explosion. I'm going to try to find it. I'll write down what I learn and read it to you.
   He's laughing.
   I laugh.

What?
Know what, Dad?
What?
She looks like a frog too. Know what Mom called you before she went?
What?
A worm.
   Even things that don't rise converge.
   We hang up.

The knowledge eminently possessed by Shakespeare is something beyond mere acquisition—the kind of knowledge that comes only to "an experiencing nature"; and the experiencing nature, like creative genius, is a gift, not an acquirement. People have made a Shakespeare "mystery" by trying to find reasons for what is beyond reason. All creative genius is a mystery, and utterly inexplicable. (258)

No, darling, I don't think I am William Shakespeare.
   I am a fastly aging man in a yellow room looking out upon the black nerves that are red in the illustration in the children's encyclopedia and wondering what bird to put on that, the sciatic nerve, in place of the one that I saw there last summer, a robin, dull and common. I like the starkness of the cardinal and they do travel about in winter and might land on such a tree. On the other hand, it may be too flashy for the purposes of this piece, though those are yet to be identified.
   The cardinal, or another bird, or perhaps the worm, will lead me beyond the building and then I will know about the building.
   Or maybe I will not.
   Half of the fun, my uncle used to say when we complained about how long it was taking to wherever we were going, *is in the getting there.*

Flatland

Morning innocence.
This is a flat town. This is a flat town whose flatness goes all ways. This is a flat town whose narrow streets turn to cornfields at the edges. This is a flat town and the faces of its people would tell you that, for the faces of the people are flat and the weather is flat, flat hot or flat cold, summer and winter falling into each other, flatly into each other.
Marcy!
An hour of miles to the north the land reaches an enormous lake that was once clean but is now becoming a swamp black with mud and debris and was always flat like the land and was the land until the land was drained and became the black mud flatness of the lake sinking into itself, darkening itself, like the flat swamp where now there are cornfields and people.
Is this our time and place, Marcy?
To the south there are hills and mountains but they are far off and broken in between only by a few trees and ribbons of concrete which rise briefly only briefly and then are reclaimed by the land and the flatness of the land which dominates and is unredeemed. Flat.

Martin's World

Do you hear me?
The park. The sun climbs up the trees.
"Squeaker! The little slide, not the big one."
She doesn't hear.
Young woman. Very thin, white face, narrow hook of a nose. Here alone? Always here alone? In this flat park with its tall trees? Did she miss a ride and get left here? Or was she always here? And haven't I seen her elsewhere, alone, walking over the dark earth alone? And would she answer if I spoke?
Answer me!
"Squeaker!"
"Where's the other?"
"Get down there and help me find your brother."
There were other girls and women. What was I trying to remember then? I don't remember. I remember falling through the days, waving my fists at the sun and thinking I carried the thoughts of the gods of my ancestors. I was out of the hospital, free for a moment. O, the women were good then and the drinks were good and my mind burst upward with possibilities. Laying my hands on the moon and crying out to the universe, I *would* be heard. I held them, the women, and the songs and the women and the drink erased the night, the black pit of night. I was surrounded. But had eyes for only one.
The children have gone. Where are the children?
"Squeaker! Bumbo!"
Ai! She looks with eyes that would invite the devil. Another who looked like her. I remember the other at the back of the classroom. Wrote poetry, someone said. And this one?
"Hello."
She turns away.
Where are my children? Does she see where my children have gone? I hear a train. Will she come to this green bench and tell me how to live on the flatness of this land? Where are my children? Can she see them beyond those trees?
Speak to me, Marcy!
She is passing beneath those trees, going off alone on this morning, withdrawing softly as if she knows the ground does not invite her. So like that other when Marcy came and met me after the class and she, the other, passed us and looked at Marcy and at me and was there, always there in morning. She sometimes smiled at me. But I didn't speak to her. And this one doesn't smile.

Marcy, you know nothing of the terror of your silence! Nothing!

This one and the other like her I would never have wanted, but Marcy I have wanted, on her terms, not mine. What are her terms?

Where are the children?

"Squeaker! Bump!"

Silence.

That one and the other and Marcy.

Marcy.

Silence.

This is a flat and silent land.

Where are the children?

Damn you, Marcy!

There are invisible extensions I cannot taste or put into words.

Ah, there in the sand box. Safe. "Get up now. We have to go."

And for what did we fight? And for what the words? The words that drain blackly into this land?

"Now Squeaker. Now!"

Marcy!

I have wound around this time before. I have wound around these thoughts in this flat land.

"The seats on that swing set are wet. Next time. Next time. We must go."

She ran out once and took the car and the police stopped her and told me she was driving recklessly and said she didn't seem to know the danger. I could have told them she hadn't spoken for days and wouldn't speak and still it goes on.

Should we hold a little longer?

She is on the living room floor. She is curled on the floor and I take the children upstairs before they see her and I put them in their room and I come down and I say, whisper, "Marcy?" Her body throbs and she is sobbing but her sobs are more than sobs for they reach down to her feet but less than sobs and soon I can't hear them. I touch her shoulder but she curls up tighter. I back away.

"Marcy," I say.

She doesn't speak.

I walk to the window and look out.

The land goes off to the north, deceiving no one. There isn't a single cloud. There are trains but I hear no trains. I see not a man or a dog or a car. I can't see the flatness because of the houses. But it is there. Always there. If I were to reach out with an infinite reach I would find nothing but the flatness. Nothing.

Night Life

It was a warm night between wars. No one had spoken loudly until Jerry said, "There are reasons to kill and don't think I wouldn't do it if someone was trying to turn my street into a dead-end."

"Give one person the right and you give everyone the right," said Glenn.

"That's true," Ginger put in. "Do you want a country full of Mansons?"

Jerry smiled. "Maybe."

A couple of them looked at me, as though I would have something illuminating to say. I didn't. I wanted the conversation to quiet down again.

After Marcy left I started taking women home with me, one, then another and another. There have been many. Two of them have the same name—Sandra. One of the Sandras suggested the party. "Summer will soon be over, and we'll all pass from each other's lives." I told her I didn't have the energy to get everything together. She said she'd take care of it.

Now Ginger said, "Where's Donald?"

"I didn't invite him," said Sandra.

I'd asked her not to. I didn't feel like telling the others that. I didn't feel like explaining.

Donald's eyes search up and down his walls when he's alone with his cats late at night. One night I stopped to visit, looked through his window, saw his eyes fall to his hands, limp on his lap, waited for him to lift his head. He didn't. Watching him killed my interest. I tiptoed off his porch and went home.

"I wish he were here." Ginger went on. "I like to hear him complain about his mother." Ginger had been studying for a master's degree but quit to concentrate on writing poetry.

"Donald is apposite," said Glenn.

In the morning the sheets smell like the last woman who's slept with me. One of the Sandras has a summer fragrance, wafts of peonies. The other's is a rich and earthy smell. I picture a wolverine. Here is a dark woman, Karla. She left her small child with its father in another state and now takes philosophy courses and works as a secretary. Hers is a tangible licorice odor, and it enters the undersheet and mattress too. Even after the sheets are washed I detect it.

"What does apposite mean?" someone asked.

"Relevant, you ass," said Glenn. He tends bar at Kavanagh's and has been, on and off, working toward a Ph.D. in linguistics.

After a dreary seminar I told Marcy, "I think many of my grad students come to the university to escape." She said she had no interest in my students or what I had to say about them. She soon went to our nearest neighbors' house. I took the children to the park. When we returned, the evening light had vanished. She was still at the neighbors'. After the children were in bed I called there. Their oldest child answered, said her parents and Marcy had gone to Friendly's for ice cream. I waited for her until I was too tired to stay up. The next day, before going to the university, I left her a note: "Must we share only silence?" She never wrote or spoke a reply.

Once, in the middle of a conversation, Donald stood and said, "I have to take a shower." He went into his bathroom and came out moments later wearing red bikini shorts with thin yellow stripes. There was flab on his white stomach, which had little hair. He started looking for something. "She ignores you, doesn't she," he said. "No," I lied. He didn't find what he was looking for. He turned at the bathroom doorway. "I have my cats," he said, each word collapsing into the next. "What else have I got?"

Glenn told us he had taken coke before coming to the party. "I always get hard easily after I snort," he said.

"Let's see." Maggie placed her hand against his penis. Quickly he grew hard.

"What did I tell you?" he said.

"You also take Vitamin E," someone reminded him. "It was probably the E." Maggie smiled. "Does it matter?"

Martin's World

"Pedantry," Jerry went on. "If we were true to ourselves we wouldn't be here. We take money for teaching freshmen how to support the fucking system. We're all liars."

"Quit then," said Glenn, who was now nibbling at Maggie's neck. "Fuck quitting," said Jerry. "I'm an anarchist. What am I supposed to do if I quit, join the police force?"

Karla had been dozing on the love seat. Her long arms stretched upward. Lowering them, she scratched her tanned stomach just above her cut-off jeans. Without turning to Jerry, she said, "Go shoot someone."

"Yourself," added Glenn.

Most would leave in two weeks when the summer session ended. Glenn and Maggie were going to Cleveland, where he'd taken a low-paying job doing publicity for a string of health spas. Sandra, a recent Master's graduate in sociology, was going to the University of Colorado to begin work on a Ph.D. Karla would stay, waitressing and taking classes that appealed to her. When Ginger wasn't helping run her family's farm in Pennsylvania, she'd attend summer writers' conferences.

The other Sandra wasn't at the party. She spent her days watching her two boys participate in track and baseball programs at the park, feeding them lunch and sending them to the city pool for the afternoon. After Marcy left with the children to her mother's farm in Nebraska, she began stopping by in the afternoons. We talked about how poor the grade school was and about work I was doing on the house and such. Once, when she was pouring me coffee she stood close and I sent my hand across her back and we embraced, then quickly kissed. It went on. We soon moved upstairs and made love rapidly with much kissing. She hadn't come to the party because she was afraid to leave her boys home alone at night.

"Something's wrong with you," Donald said. "Marcy's completely unsympathetic. Don't you know that. She's going to leave you. I'll do whatever you want, Martin. If you want to have women in my extra bedroom, you can have them."

Jerry went on talking. I listened and didn't listen. There was a letter somewhere in the house. Where had I put it? Sometimes I hid distasteful correspondence from myself—requests for letters of recommendation from former students, bills I didn't want to pay. I'd find them days later, finally do what was asked. This letter was from Marcy. I'd found nothing hopeful in it. Maybe, on a second reading, I would.

Karla remained in the soft chair watching as the others departed.

After I'd seen the last of them to the door, I went behind the chair and pulled her long hair tightly back, squeezing until it felt hard. She liked me doing that. She liked rough gestures. I told her I'd ask her to stay but was too preoccupied to relax. I released her hair. She got up and moved to the door but lingered there. "I don't want to go." I pushed her tight against the door jamb and kissed her hard, the way she liked. She moved against me. I wasn't aroused. I pulled back, said "Sorry, I can't. There's something, a letter I have to find, then figure out." She gave me a disappointed shrug and looked at her watch. Kavanagh's would still be open.

I looked for a couple of hours but didn't find the letter.

PHILIP F. O'CONNOR is a native of San Francisco and a graduate of San Francisco State College and the University of Iowa. In 1970 he founded the Creative Writing Program at Ohio's Bowling Green State University, where he is now a Distinguished Professor emeritus.

His award-winning short stories in *Old Morals, Small Continents, Darker Times* (Univ. of Iowa Press, 1971) and *A Season for Unnatural Causes* (University of Illinois, 1975) won this praise from novelist Stanley Elkins: "Excellent, written throughout with a sort of honed dignity which does credit to the author's kindly passion and gentle intelligence."

His best-selling novel, *Stealing Home* (Knopf, 1980), set in a Midwestern small town, was critically acclaimed and a National Book Award finalist. Webster Schott described it in the *New York Times*: "*Stealing Home* is extraordinary: a novel that seriously examines difficult questions about human motive and need."

His second novel, *Defending Civilization* (Weidenfeld & Nicolson, 1988), won this recognition from Paul West: "I can tell how well Philip O'Connor knows the off-duty military mind; his novel is hilarious, upsetting, and a great encouragement to sanity. He writes with a tonic sparkle and a loving eye for the inane."

Finding Brendan (Summit Books, 1991) has been described by novelist Dan O'Brien as "a delightful example of a mature writer taking on a difficult subject. O'Connor rises to the challenge with compassion and the clever use of the tools of his trade. The result is an extraordinary novel."

The stories in *Martin's World* were originally composed during 1961-1975. In them, Philip F. O'Connor listens to the landscape of people and places. His writing has always located us in the midst of our consciousness of life.

A Well of Living Water

Annabel Thomas

*"Whosoever drinketh of this water shall thirst again;
But whosoever drinketh of the water that I shall give him
shall never thirst; but the water that I shall give him
shall be in him a well of water springing up into everlasting life."
The woman saith unto Him, "Sir, give me this water."*
St. John 4:14-15

"A fountain of gardens, a well of living waters."
The Song of Solomon 4:15

© copyright 1993
Annabel Thomas
A Well of Living Water
ISBN 0-933087-27-6

The author would like to acknowledge the following
publications which first published these stories:

"The Westerer" in Prairie Schooner 1975
"Jonquils" in The Ohio Review 1985
"Twister" in Forum (Ball State University) 1974
"Margaret and Erdine" in The Literary Review 1978
"Wellspring" in Forum 1979

"Twister," "Margaret and Erdine" and "Wellspring"were also part of the short story collection *The Phototropic Woman* (University of Iowa Press, 1981)

BOOK I   BUDDY

Part I   The Westerer

1.

Queen had a bay like a church bell. Buddy would have loved to lay his head on her chest when she gave tongue so as to hear the sound come clanging up out of her, but she was off and running like the Devil had her tail between his teeth.

"Ululul," she went and Buddy went "ululul" but not so much like a bell and romped pell-mell after her.

Panting, Buddy caught her up and found her stopped by a pool where water trickled down over greenish rock. Buddy's papa came up behind walking heavy with big boots.

"She's run it into its den," Papa said. "Good girl, Queenie. Good old bitch. Look at her dig, Bud."

Buddy scooted on his knees up behind the hound and peered into the hole in the bank. Queen, her muddy tongue dripping saliva, looked up into Buddy's face, yelped, and began to dig again with a strong frantic scratching of her front toenails.

Papa sat down on a stone and pushed back his cap.

"What is it?" Buddy asked.

"Possum."

"Queen'll bring it up to us, won't she?"

A Well of Living Water

"Maybe. That den's an old one. The possum's way down in the ground. Might be we'll have to give it up. Still, she may fetch it. If the den ain't got another door."

Queenie worked like a demon widening the mouth of the hole. Buddy could scarcely believe his eyes. Sleepy old Queenie. Then down the hole she went. Ten minutes later she backed out, dirty as sin, limped to the pool and drank with a noisy lapping.

"Her foot's bleeding!" Buddy said in a hushed voice.

"She's tore her nails digging. She's hitting some rocks."

"She pants so awful. Let's call her off."

"No. She's doing all right. You stay here. I'm going back and get the pickax."

Buddy watched his papa disappear amongst the bone-white trunks of the trees. There was no sound but the water dripping down the rocks.

When Queen came up for another drink, Buddy called to her but she never looked around. It was as if she didn't know him from Adam.

Papa strode back carrying the pick over his shoulder. They heard Queen yelp down in the ground. Papa knelt by the hole.

"Here, Queenie," he called and his voice was deep and booming in the quiet.

The dog yelped again. Then she came out, scrambling and scratching, her face bloody and her eyes wild.

"She caught up with the rascal," Papa said. "It's bit her there on the muzzle. Notice them marks?"

Buddy laughed to see Queen stick her smarting nose into the cool water of the pool. Then she drank in eager gulps.

Papa began to dig, swinging the pick easily up over his shoulder and down again. Queen jumped at his heels, turning herself around this way and that way, wanting to be digging, too. When he got tired, Papa let her go down. He leaned on the pick, listening to her scratch underground.

Buddy watched his father pull out his pipe and stick it between his teeth where it bobbed as he packed it with tobacco. He let Buddy light it.

"How've those women been keeping their health since I was home last?" Papa asked in his rumbly voice, not looking at Buddy.

"Gramma's back aches her some."

"Do the women talk of me, ever?"

"Yes."

"Do they make you afraid of me?"

"No. They just say you drink. And stay away from home."

"That first is a lie. I don't take liquor scarcely at all when I'm selling on the road. Only here at home."

Papa pulled the pipe from between his teeth, laughed shortly and spat expertly into the pool.

"However," he continued, "I own I don't come back here as much as I might. What do you think of that?"

"Why don't you?"

"Ha, ha. You're one what strikes to the core of the matter, I see. I don't know you, boy. What are you now, ten? You've growed up and I don't know you."

Buddy watched his father's Adam's apple while he talked. It went up and down and hair grew in the hollow beneath it.

"I'll tell you why I stay away. I can't stand to live in your Gramma Wheat's house."

"Why not?"

"Because a house is only big enough for one live man, not a live one and a dead one."

Papa suddenly raised the pick and brought it down into the ground with a force that sunk it to the handle.

"Now think, Buddy. What does Gramma say about Grampa?"

"She says, 'Pretty soon he'll come walking in that front door.'"

"That's it. That's exactly it. She's bound he's coming back!"

"Mama thinks so too."

"Yes. Your mama is the same. Your Gramma Wheat tells her what to think and Mama, she thinks it. That's the truth."

"Don't you believe Grampa is coming back?"

"Did you ever see a dead person, Buddy?"

"No."

"They get stiff as iron and cold as stone. After you bury them down in the ground their skin rots off and the worms eat their eyes. If you was to dig them up after a few years you wouldn't find nothing but just bones."

Buddy's mouth opened of itself.

"And if Gramma Wheat waits until the last breath of her life, she'll never see that day that old Garth's bones is going to get up out of that cemetery plot and march in the door.

"I for one ain't going to live there and watch that idiot old woman wait for him to come." Papa's voice rattled echoes out of the rocks far down the hollow.

"It's Garth done it this way, and Garth done it that until I can't take a breath or eat a egg or shit if it wasn't the way Garth done it. That's why I don't come home. A dead man belongs under the ground, not up with the living."

Buddy listened with his jaw dropped down. He had never heard his father say so much on any subject.

While Papa talked, it had grown steadily darker. Now a mist of rain began to

A Well of Living Water

sift down on them through the branches. Queen's muffled scratching and whining had been sounding all along from down in the den. Suddenly her voice rose piercingly in yelp upon yelp. Buddy and his father jumped to their feet.

Papa pulled up the pickax from where he had buried it in the earth and began to dig rapidly, widening the den's mouth, spewing dirt to left and right. He tore off his coat and threw it down on the rocks and recommenced digging.

"She's caught up with that possum again," he cried over his shoulder. "Listen to her yell. By god, it's slit her throat."

Buddy peered into the den between his father's legs.

"Here she comes," he sang out in wonder.

For old Queen's rump appeared wiggling now this way, now that as she backed up out of the hole. Papa threw down the pick and, laying hold of her hind legs, hauled the dog out with one powerful swing of his arms.

"Good girl! She's got it! Look at there, Buddy, she's hauled it along with her. She's bit its jugular in two. What do you think about that?"

Queen, being set down, growled fiercely and backed off, shaking her head, so that the animal in her mouth flopped to and fro.

"Drop that now. Leave loose, you damned old rip," Papa shouted, cuffing her smartly along the jaw. "She's ruint the pelt a'ready."

Queen opened her mouth enough for Papa to jerk the possum away from her. She whined, jumping up and up again toward the carcass dangling over her head.

"Got a nice thick coat on it," Papa said, blowing back the hair. "We'll take it along home and stretch it. I may be able to trim it up to sell."

"Come on along," Papa said, turning away. "It's going to cut loose and rain us out. I'll take the pickax. You tote the possum."

They made their way up the bank and along the ridge in a soft whisper of rain. They went single file through the darkening woods; first Queen, then Papa, then Buddy. It was a good three miles back to Trent.

Buddy hadn't ever touched a dead animal. He held the hind paws clamped gingerly between his knuckles. The weight of the body hit against his knees at each step.

At first the possum was still warm. Its eyes were half open and it had a queer little smile. Buddy could see sharp teeth under its lifted lip.

Slowly, as he walked on, the blood dried at its throat and it began to stiffen and grow cold. Queen came back and nosed the possum. She wasn't much interested in it anymore. When she panted, Buddy saw she had its blood still on her tongue.

The stiffer the possum got, the colder grew its paws. Feeling the possum's awful coldness, Buddy began to shiver. He carried it for a while longer; then,

A Well of Living Water

lagging behind so his father wouldn't see, he let it drop like a stone into the leaves.

The farther he moved from where the possum lay, the faster he went until he was tearing along stumbling over roots, with his breath whistling in his windpipe.

The woods had begun to thin out before Buddy slowed his pace. He went on at a walk, rubbing his hands on his shirt. All around him the rain was falling with a sighing sound.

2.

There were days when Buddy hated his Gramma Wheat because she made him the laughingstock of Kimball County.

Every soul in Trent and for miles round the countryside knew she expected her husband to return from the dead and take over the farm.

"I seen your grampa last night," the children told Buddy at school. "He was sitting on his tombstone picking his teeth with a coffin nail. He said he wasn't going to come back till the price of corn goes up ten cents to the bushel."

Every day they had a new joke to tell. Buddy gave and got blackened eyes and bloodied noses, and still the jokes went on. He ended by keeping to himself.

In spring and summer he helped his mama, Enid, make garden. In the fall they planted jonquil bulbs. She dearly loved her plants, but she was delicate and her arms got tired. Buddy soon grew taller than she was so that he looked down on her dark hair and down into her thin face that was always smiling.

Sometimes when Gramma Wheat's back hurt, he helped her clean the floors, but he could never scrub hard enough to please her.

Best of all he liked to be with his papa. During the long stretches when Art Hilder was away selling on the road, Buddy grew restless. He moved about the tumbledown farm like a lick of flame in a burnt-out log, always listening for the sound of his papa's car.

When his papa came home in hunting season of Buddy's twelfth year, Buddy became rich in rabbit tails. Papa shot rabbits in the brush during the day and cleaned them by the back porch in full sight of the kitchen windows while the women were fixing supper. He threw the heads and entrails into the yard for Queen.

"These rascals is long gone," he said loudly. "Ain't none of these rascals coming back on Judgment Day."

At night he drank whiskey in the empty shed and sang songs. After he had been home a week, Gramma Wheat got heart palpitations and had to breathe with her mouth open.

A Well of Living Water

Sometimes when Buddy went to tell his mama and papa goodnight, the bedroom was locked and he could hear them arguing and discussing behind the closed door. Sometimes he heard whispers and giggles.

Every day Mama smiled as usual, but Papa scowled and Gramma Wheat went about her work with a pink spot in the middle of each freckled cheek. She had been red-headed when she was young, and she still had a red-headed woman's temper.

Watching them all, Buddy couldn't find a place to rest anywhere in the house. Each day the ceilings felt heavier, as if the family were in a balloon and the air leaking out.

On the last grey Saturday in November, Papa packed his gear, washed, shaved himself of a two weeks' beard and had a new battery put into his car.

He stood in the door with his coat buttoned over his thick chest and his hat slapped onto the back of his head. He smelt of axle grease, shaving lotion and rye whiskey.

"Enid," he said, "come along with me. You and Bud."

"Now?"

"I been telling you."

"But the boy's in school." She spoke in a hushed voice, twisting her hands one in the other and glancing at Buddy sitting on the stairs and at Gramma Wheat out in her kitchen rocker.

"There's schools in California. I thought you'd come at last, Enid."

"I can't just pack up and go, like you can, Art."

"Why not? Why the hell not?"

Buddy saw his mama begin to perspire at the temples. Her hair grew damp where it curled back over her small ears.

"If you're bound to take this job so far away, maybe Buddy and I can come out later. This summer when his school's done. When Ma's got better of her heart spell."

"Later be damned, Enid! It's now or never. You know it. I know it. Are you or ain't you coming?"

She wet her lips. "You know I can't leave Ma," she said in a low voice.

"Then bring her along."

"You know she won't come. She's waiting here on Dad."

Papa stood big as an ox in the doorway shutting out the daylight. The room was growing cold.

"I won't be back, Enid."

"I know. You said so. I know."

"Come with me."

There he stood, big as a mountain. Gramma Wheat sat silent in her rocker.

A Well of Living Water

Buddy thought, 'Mama's like a bone with Papa and Gramma Wheat pulling at her.' He wanted Papa to win.

He plugged his ears with his fingers and screwed his eyes tight shut. When he opened his eyes, his mama was standing alone in the room. The front door banged in the wind.

Buddy ran out the door, but Papa's car was gone from the drive. He ran back to the house and mounted the stairs, still running. He burst into Grampa Wheat's bedroom.

The bay window commanded the road for a good mile out of town. Buddy raised the blinds. There went the green car over the first hill. He waited. It reappeared and dropped over the top of the second hill. Well, he was gone. There was no catching him.

The chance of going to California was gone, the chance of getting away from Gramma Wheat and her sharp tongue and from his teasing schoolmates. Papa was gone over the second hill and Buddy hadn't even said good-bye.

The afternoon sun came in strong at the window. He saw his mother standing in the hall watching him.

"Draw Grampa's blinds," she told him. "Gramma don't want the rug to fade."

3.

As the months went by, Papa wrote less and less often, each time from a different town. The letters Mama sent were mailed back unopened because he had already moved on.

Mama was sick during the winter. Buddy had to come straight home from school each evening to help her with her work.

He knew she liked to sit in the sunny kitchen window watching for him to walk up the road when school let out. He brought her presents: a pocketful of black walnuts, a rounded stone, a handful of herbs. They sat with their heads together over the table while he ate his snack and told her all he had seen that day. When she baked bread, they split the warm heel between them.

Soon after Buddy turned thirteen, he got his first suit of clothes to wear to confirmation. There was much discussion in the house about the price of the suit. Papa sent less money as time went on. Enid suggested cutting down one of Grampa Wheat's suits for Buddy, but Gramma Wheat tightened her lips and shook her head.

Every Monday morning Gramma took out Grampa Wheat's two dark suits, his one white Palm Beach suit and his two pairs of grey slacks, brushed them, turned down the cuffs and hung them outside on the line to air.

The Monday after Mama thought of cutting a suit down for Buddy, Gramma Wheat's fingers trembled as she brushed the clothes and she hung them out fiercely and arranged the folds with angry and watchful looks. Enid, weeping for shame, took money from her small savings and bought the suit and there was peace in the house.

At confirmation, Buddy's mama and Gramma Wheat stood up with him. After the service, Gramma Wheat said, "Praise Jesus, Buddy. Now you got eternal life."

Mama smiled and kissed him.

The congregation shook hands with the confirmation class. Each member got a Bible and a certificate. On the back of Buddy's certificate one of the other children had scribbled, 'Your mama's in a family way!'

In the spring, Enid's small feet and ankles began to swell and she lay on her bed all day. Buddy brought her narcissus, then jonquils, lilac, then moss rosebuds ready to burst open.

She thanked him, but her eyes picked over the flowers as if she were searching for some other blossom he hadn't brought. Her face was no longer thin but round as a moon and altogether strange.

She started into labor late at night. Buddy was jolted from his bed by her screams. He ran out into the hall. There Gramma Wheat stood with her sandy-grey hair loose down her back.

"Was that Mama hollered out?"

"She's birthing the baby."

"Does it hurt her so much?"

"Yes."

"Will it take very long?"

"A body can't tell as to that."

"Is Doctor Joe in there?"

"Yes. Him and his missus both. I telephoned right after eleven."

Through the night, Mama went on screaming. Now and again she called out Papa's name.

At daybreak, Buddy put on his clothes and went out of the house. All that day he went in and out, in and out. Gramma Wheat kept the shades pulled and the doors shut. The house smelt queer and everyone whispered.

In the evening, Buddy gave Queen her supper in the yard. When he came in he stood a long time listening in the lower hall. A change had come over the house. He could not say what it was, but the short hairs rose on his neck.

Upstairs a door slammed open and strong light fell out into the hall. Pans

A Well of Living Water

rattled briskly and people talked in strange harsh voices.

Buddy climbed the stairs. Doctor Joe Bryant, white-haired and big-stomached, came hurrying out with a handful of medicines, both bottles and envelopes. He set the medicines down on a chair and struck his hands impatiently against his thighs.

"There you are, boy," he said in a loud discontented voice. "We've been calling for you. Didn't you hear? You've got a brother."

"Mama?"

"She went into a fit. Eclampsia. You knew she had kidney trouble?"

"No."

"I told her another pregnancy would likely kill her. Told her plain as I'm telling you, boy. I done all I could. She's only just died. We was calling you."

"She's dead?"

"Yes. I'm sorry. But there it is. You must be a man about it. I want to get her out of the house as soon as possible. Your Gramma Wheat is out of her head. In shock and so on. I gave her a sedative. She's sitting in there now. She's quiet. You'll have to buck up and look after her. Can you do that?"

Doctor Joe gave Buddy a sharp look.

"Yes sir."

"She was odd when Garth died, too. I want to get your mother right out of here. You understand?"

"Yes sir."

"I've been telephoning Partlow, and I can't get him. Likely he's over at the pool room. You know the place? Yes. Well, I must go on to another patient, but I'll write a note. You take it to Partlow. Hunt him up and hand him this note. He'll send the hearse around. Then you take this prescription to the drug store and get it filled for your gramma. The Missus will stay here until you get back."

When he brought the medicine home, they had cleared out Mama's room. She was gone. The bed was made up as if she had never laid in it. His Great Aunt Lou Fowler, with her bright blue eyes and round cheeks, met him at the door and kissed him. Somewhere back in the house, a baby was crying.

4.

Enid Hilder's funeral was held Sunday afternoon in the church. Buddy wore his new suit. Although his gramma sent off a lot of telegrams to many places, Buddy's papa couldn't be reached, so Buddy and Gramma Wheat were chief mourners. There was a sizable crowd since the weather was fine.

A good many friends and relatives came back to the house to sit and talk

A Well of Living Water

afterwards. Some of them took supper before going home. When at last the house was clear of visitors, Buddy took off his suit and folded the pants carefully across a hanger.

Aunt Lou Fowler and Gramma Wheat sat in the parlor. His gramma still had on her black shantung, although she had tied her apron over it and slipped off her shoes. Buddy stood at the parlor window in the draining light staring out into the yard where Queenie was chewing a bone.

After a time, the street lights came on and the parlor fell into shadow. Gramma Wheat cleared her throat.

"Now that was a fine funeral," she said. Buddy heard her chair squeak as she settled her crippled back into the pillow. "It took a good piece of our savings but it was a fine service."

"The coffin cost too much," Aunt Lou said.

"Yes, it did. But it was metal. And the handles was polished brass. Partlow said no water gets in metal. They was twenty-one baskets of flowers. I mind Garth had thirty-six, but twenty-one is nothing to be ashamed of. There must have been a hundred people came up and shook my hand at the cemetery. They was most as many as come when you buried yore boys, Lou."

"Most as many," Aunt Lou agreed.

"Enid looked real pretty. Partlow had her fixed nice, considering what she'd passed through." Gramma Wheat blew her nose.

Buddy moved back from the window. "He rouged her cheeks," Buddy said. "She didn't even look dead until you got up close."

Up close, Buddy thought, you could see Mama had the same queer little smile as the possum.

"Yore mama's only sleeping, Buddy," Gramma Wheat said. "She's got her a perfect body in the Lord and she'll wake up and come back to us on that 'Great Getting-Up Morning' as they calls it. God's going to lead her back. She'll come walking in that very door. Her and Garth together. You'll see. It'll happen while we're still alive here."

Buddy stood before Gramma Wheat with his chin stuck out.

"At the cemetery," he said in a stubborn voice, "I walked over and looked down the shaft. Did you? I seen the mud walls and they went down a mile. I watched them men of Partlow's lower the box and shovel dirt onto it. Pounds and pounds of dirt. It must be cold as Christmas down there. And blacker than midnight without no moon nor stars out.

"Ain't no way I can see that Mama is going to get up out of that grave hole, Gramma. Ain't no way."

"You're a young boy and don't understand the ways of the Lord."

"Papa says when a person's dead, they're dead and you'd just as well put up with it."

"Yore Papa ain't no Christian," Gramma Wheat cried out, jumping up and stamping her foot. "And neither are you if you go on this way." Her face burned red and she went into the kitchen, barefoot, and began putting the food away, banging the kettles and dishes so loud they sent rattles through every room in the house.

"Now, Buddy, come here," Aunt Lou Fowler said, and she pulled him onto her lap where she was sitting in the oak rocker and laid his head on her shoulder. His legs hung down like a colt's, but she was a big woman and her lap was soft and he let her rock him while she talked into his ear.

"When me and your gramma was little girls," Aunt Lou said, "Gramma went with two of her friends to take their daddies' lunches down mine. When they came to a low beam in one of the shafts, they set by the lunch pails and swung on it. The second swing it broke and the roof come down on all three. Yore gramma's back was hurt. The two other little girls laid there half under the dirt and timber. Gramma shook them and talked to them but they never answered. She laid there alone in the dark with them hours and hours. She like to never got out. It was two days before the miners found her.

"That was a awful thing for yore gramma, Buddy, to catch such a sharp sight of death and her so young. Now I'll tell you another tale.

"You mind my house, don't you, up on Fowler's Mountain by the windmill that used to scare you when you was a shaver? In that house I borned two boys you never knowed, Buddy. My boys used to go swimming bare-ass in the crick when they was about yore age.

"One day Chester got a cramp so's he couldn't keep afloat. Down he went head under and come up threshing around hunting for something to hang onto to save hisself. He grabbed hold of Asa and drug him down, too, and they both didn't come up no more.

"Yore gramma does like Chester done. She's a fighter by nature. She's been threshing and grabbing all her life. Now you're all she's got left, Buddy. You got to stand firm for her to hold onto if you can, but don't let her pull you under."

Buddy held his face against Aunt Lou Fowler's shoulder. After a long while he said, muffled and low, "Don't you pine awful for Chester and Asa, Aunt Lou?"

"Yes, I do," she answered him. "Still, there's times I feel they're hanging around me yet. I can hug you because I hugged them first. Besides, now I'm taking the little'un to raise, I'll have me a boy again. But you must keep close with yore brother, Buddy," she said, "as the day'll likely come you'll be all he's got in this world. You'll be yore brother's keeper, as the Good Book has it.

"Now you trot out into the kitchen and help yore gramma clear up just like you used to help yore mama, and that'll be a step along the way."

But when Buddy stood by the table, he saw that Gramma Wheat had placed his mama's gardening shoes beneath the bench in the corner. They were small and scuffed, worn over at the sides and pointed in at the toes. Dirt still clung to the edges of the heels. There they sat, ready for her to put them on, and it was more than he could bear.

He picked up the shoes, opened the door, and threw them as far as he could, one and then the other, out beyond the porch into the yard.

"Where're you going to, Buddy?" Gramma Wheat called after him as he stepped off the porch.

"I'm going to find Papa," he said. "I'm going to California."

He set off in a straight line through backyards and alleys toward the hills where the sun had set. When he came to open country, he kept on by moonlight across new-plowed fields and pasture, through wood lots, over fences and small runs of water.

He heard the screech of owls and crickets' chirring and frogs' singing. Now and then a wild animal started up from under his feet and dashed away, but he never saw what kind it was.

Only when he began to weave and stumble over nothing, he realized he was played out. Each time he fell it was harder to get up. His knees hurt from scraping the ground. His shirt, soaked with sweat, stuck to his chest and his breath sawed in and out of his throat.

He wandered into a farmyard where a machine shed and two barns stood. He crept into the nearest barn and sat down on the floor, his arms and legs trembling and his teeth clicking together. The barn smelled of sheep.

His eyelids grew heavy in the warmth of the straw and his head nodded. Before he slept, he thought that in California he would live with his papa and he would own a bicycle. He would go to a school where nobody knew him and become a basketball star or a runner of the low hurdles. Summers, he would help Papa sell. They would go on the road together and neither of them would ever die.

Part II   Jonquils

1.

On the day Buddy's mama had been buried one month, Gramma Wheat said, "Yore papa's dead though he walks the streets in Californy, whilst yore mama lives though she lies still in her grave."

It wasn't until the next spring that Buddy grasped what Gramma had in mind.

He was digging in his mama's jonquil bed making a hole to plant a white rosebush. The jonquils' green foliage was shooting up lushly so that he was able to choose an empty spot in which to place the rose.

Deep and deeper he sent his spade into cold earth beginning to soften so that it clumped and clung to the spade's metal tip. Of a sudden he brought up a strange brown thing, twisted and rotted, like a lump of chewed tobacco.

Buddy took it between his fingers: an empty sack, worm-riddled. He dropped the spade and crouched staring at the shriveled shell lying on his muddy palm. And only when he touched it again with his fingertips and recognized it as a jonquil bulb did he understand that this bulb was Papa's soul, while the others were Mama's, sprouting green toward God out of a short winter's death.

Afterward, throughout his boyhood, Buddy was good for his mama, Enid's sake, for the sake of greeting her at last in Beulah Land.

A Well of Living Water

Left alone together, Buddy and Gramma Wheat managed to live in tolerable harmony. At sixteen, Buddy quit school and hired himself out to farmers round about. Of an evening, Gramma always had a hot supper waiting on him, and now and again special treats: a blackberry cobbler or an apple turnover, sugared, and cream poured over it.

"Yore gramma shorely dotes on you, boy," their neighbors told him.

But Buddy knew better. More often than not, she was cranky and snappish. She made him scrub his muddy boots. She fussed at him if the water bucket stood empty. She sent him to chop a stack of wood when he was dead tired. And every chore he did on the place set her tongue clacking as to how Grampa had done it a better way.

Still, she was such a funny, dear, wrinkled-up-hump-backed little thing and so spunky that he enjoyed her. She made him laugh. By the time he was seventeen, he could pick her up off the floor and swing her about. He teased her and humored her and gave her always a kiss goodnight.

As Buddy grew older, the urge to go traveling came strong and stronger on him. It swelled and itched and smoldered until it wouldn't be denied. At last the notion took him to join the army and see the wide world.

When he talked of enlisting, Gramma went about the house stiff and clenched in every muscle, so set was she against his going from home. She clamped her mouth into a line and wouldn't give him the time of day. Or else she loosed her tongue until he grew weary of its sound.

"You'll fall into evil ways, do you go a-soldiering," she said. "You'll commence living the sporting life: whiskey-drinking, blaspheming, chasing after wild women, smoking stogies and opified cigarettes and gaming, besides the doughboy's business of killing and maiming other human creatures. 'Thou shalt not,' says the Lord yore God. You'll shorely lose yore soul, Buddy, like what yore papa done when he left Enid and went off to Californy."

Buddy snickered. "Ain't you heard the war's over, old woman?" he said and tickled her neck. "No killing a-tall going on now. For the rest, I'll just say 'nothankee.'"

And he kept on and on about it until at last she gave in and signed the paper that let him go.

Waiting on the time to leave, he prattled gaily, building air castles, making plans so that his voice bounced off the ceilings and the walls and echoed out through the yard. But his little gramma twisted her lips to one side as if she'd sucked a lemon and did the best she could, he thought, by look and by word, to spoil his pleasure.

However, when the departure hour came at last, Gramma Wheat surprised

A Well of Living Water

him by traveling down to the railroad station to see him off.

Gramma, standing amongst a crowd of new recruits, dwarfed by them to child's size, dressed in a black frock and a bonnet with a black feather, surprised Buddy again by pushing a sack lunch into his hands.

Then he was on the train, laughing and waving and his heart beating high under his Adam's apple and thumping in his ears like a bass drum because he was going out into the wide world.

As he leant from the window, their eyes met, Gramma Wheat's and Buddy's, and for a moment he froze with alarm because such an odd look came on her face that it puzzled and astounded him; but the next moment she grinned and flittered her handkerchief at him and her eyes crinkled and shone bright and sunny, so that he laughed aloud again to be going on the train and made her a salute.

When, later, eating the lunch she'd packed him, he recalled her strange look, he thought it likely her back had given her a twinge as she turned to wave him farewell.

2.

On the whole, Buddy didn't mind boot camp. He'd lived in a house of women so long, he was glad to be at last a man amongst men. The army reminded him of the days before his papa had quit coming home, when they'd gone hunting together.

Buddy trained for an engineer in Washington State, and afterwards went on a troop ship across the Pacific Ocean. Every day on the water, more and more of the men spent their time shooting craps on blankets spread over the decks; joking, bragging, baiting one another as they threw the dice down. Before long, Buddy heard fellows who'd never said 'shit' in training swearing like muleskinners. Two men caught cheating were cut with knives during the crossing, and it was rumored that a heavy winner was shoved overboard and drowned. Buddy, cautious and watchful, took no part in the gaming, but instead kept to himself.

When at last they arrived at their base in Japan, Buddy was disappointed. No exotic landscape. No bomb holes or torn buildings. Just ordinary flat plains, stretching to far-off hills. The base itself was treeless. The barracks was unpainted, cold and damp. It looked like every other army base he'd ever seen, and not at all like part of the wide world.

Still, his work was exciting. He ran a power shovel. Pulling the levers, he felt as if his own arm had grown so mighty he could reach out and pick up tons of earth

A Well of Living Water

at one grab. He sent Gramma Wheat a picture of himself and his shovel. Later he mailed her a snapshot of the barracks with the window nearest his bunk marked 'X.'

The second week on the base, Buddy got a native helper, a skinny little fellow who came to work in patched coveralls.

Buddy tried his best to make friends, but the Japanese kept his face so blank it looked frozen. He seldom spoke. When he did, he sounded to Buddy like a squirrel chattering.

On the Saturday night his first overseas pass came through, Buddy was hurrying toward the barracks when a commotion broke out behind him. He swung round to find his helper pounding pell-mell after him across the yard.

The little man, wooden-faced as ever, caught hold of Buddy's arm, jabbering on and on, until Buddy began to think something awful had happened. When at last he made out he'd only broken a windshield wiper off his truck, Buddy laughed.

"Why, they's no call to carry on," he said soothingly, "I'll see it's fixed good as new in the morning."

Satisfied, his helper turned and walked quickly off, but he'd taken up so much time that when Buddy got back to the barracks, the men going into the nearest village were already dressed and on their way. They went whooping by the showers, then shouting past the windows until their voices were swallowed up in the roar of the jeep exhaust.

Buddy discovered he wasn't alone when he came on Nose Jaccaud standing by his footlocker. Water, dripping from his clothes and his hair, was making a puddle round about him on the floor. Buddy stepped back as Nose shook himself.

"They threw me in the shower," Nose explained.

He was a tall, skinny-shanked boy with pinkish hair, a tremendous nose, and eyes, Buddy thought, for all the world like a sick sheep's.

While Buddy watched, Nose reached inside his shirt and pulled out a soggy envelope. He removed three pages from it, separated them, and tried to blot them with a dry handkerchief.

"That from yore sweetpatootie?" Buddy asked.

Nose blushed and shook his head. He hung the pages over the end of his bunk like socks on a clothesline.

"This here's from Father Donahue," he said. "He's a priest I know. I used to help him weed his garden."

Buddy pulled off his shirt and rummaged in his footlocker for a clean one.

"When I was little," Nose said, "Father Donahue would stick up for me when the other kids deviled me like the fellers do here."

Buddy sat down on his bunk and rested a hand on each knee, considering.

"It bothers you so much is why they can't help but do it," he said. "Was you to act like it warn't no sweat off yore ass what they done to you, they'd leave you be."

Nose wrung out his shirttail like a dishrag.

"Onct I told Father Donahue," he said, "only way to stop folks being mean one to another'd be to keep 'em in separate slots like they do eggs."

While Buddy slid a khaki tie under his collar, Nose went sloshing over to the window beside his bunk and came back carrying a dirt-filled clay pot. He tipped it toward Buddy shyly, showing him a green shoot.

"Father Donahue sent me a bean out'n his garden," said Nose. "'Plant it, George,' he writes me, 'and when you see it growing, it'll remind you I'm sitting here thinking about your ugly mug,'"

Nose laughed, took off his left shoe and poured water from it into the pot. Buddy got to his feet and ambled off down the long row of bunks. When he reached the door, he looked back.

Nose was still standing under the light, shivering in his wet clothes, holding the bean plant. Around him, the room was full of shadow. When Buddy waved his hand, Nose raised the plant toward him in a gesture of salute as if he were preparing to drink it.

3.

Outside, the air was cold and sharp. Buddy crossed the yard and skirted the work area where his company was building an airstrip for bombers. Here, day by day, they plowed but never planted. Mounds of dirt were already ripped up and scraped away. He passed by the heavy equipment, the shovels and dozers standing silent, dirt clinging to their parts in the starshine.

When he reached the village, Buddy felt let down. A few flimsy houses set flush with the street, a few ragged people hurrying along with their eyes lowered, that was all.

He walked around until he met two soldiers from his platoon, Newell and Johnson. They were tramping the narrow street, singing loud enough to deafen the Devil. The sound of their boots on the frozen mud rang out like the reports of rifles and echoed from the unpainted fronts of the dark, shut-up buildings.

"I'll be goddamned if here ain't little Buddy Hilder come to town!" Newell cried out. "Have a drink, Hilder. Be a man. Happens I've got a bottle. Have a small snifter."

A Well of Living Water

"No thanks."

"We are on our way," continued Newell, forming his words carefully, "to a Geisha House."

"Naw, it ain't," Big Dick Johnson said.

"To a Geisha House."

"It's just a plain old cat house."

"Geisha House," Newell repeated, immovable, using his long upper lip prominently in shaping the word 'Geisha.' "You can come along, Hilder."

"Much obliged."

"We've been to a fire, Hilder," Johnson said, leaning his high frame down toward his shorter companions.

"One hell of a fire."

"What burned?"

"You know Jerry O'Malley?"

"Yes."

"He tried to burn down this gook girl's house because she gave him a dose."

"Best fire I ever saw. Spread like sixty."

"Burned up a hell of a lot of gooks, I think."

"We cut out when the MPs come. O'Malley had blew, too, so they hadn't nobody to pin it on."

"Here's the place," Newell called out in his shrill voice.

They took off their shoes on the steps of the house and ducked into a small dingy room bare of furniture. Buddy saw a number of young girls kneeling in a circle on the rice straw matting that covered the floor.

"Here's my girl, Susie-san," Newell cried. "They're all named Ruthie-san or Sally-san or Susie-san. This one of mine don't understand no English. Hey, honey, I killed your brother."

The girl, very young, with a moon face, giggled and nodded, coming up to them with tiny running steps.

"God but they giggle. Don't they giggle, Johnson? They're great gigglers."

"Get Ruthie-san for Hilder," Johnson said.

They sat down on the rice straw mat. The girls giggled. The room was cold and damp. An open charcoal fire burning in the center put out next to no heat. Buddy felt chilled to his marrow. His head commenced to ache.

He watched the girls. They were small-boned and dark, reminding him of Enid, his mama. Even their eyes seemed to him dulled as hers had been in her last days. They had on cheap-looking kimonos with wide sleeves.

Newell stood, pulled Susie-san to her feet and walked with her to a hanging bamboo partition. The two disappeared from sight.

Buddy stared into the fire. He thought the girl, with her full sleeves of colored silk, had looked like a captured butterfly as Newell jerked her along.

Buddy stood up. The girls followed his movements, giggling and fluttering. An older woman ran up to him and asked him in Pidgin English if there was a girl in the room to his liking. He shook his head and went out, replaced his shoes, and stood waiting for the others.

A flake of snow brushed his face. He had never felt so frozen. A few people passed along the street.

In the light from a store window on the corner, an old man crouched humped over against the wind, working away with his hands. Buddy stepped toward him. He knelt there, curled over like a fetus, working and working. Buddy saw that he was cutting silhouettes from black paper. He was snipping out likenesses of the people that passed by, offering them instantly for sale, dropping them at his feet if they were refused.

Buddy leaned against the corner of a building, watching the old man. He wore a dark, stained coat. His yellow puckered face had the look of one who knows secrets. Buddy stared at the cutouts on the ground, the many blank outlines of faces. He tried to move away, but he was held by the man's long dirty fingers turning and turning the black paper.

Buddy pulled his collar around his ears. His own fingers were blue with cold. He stuck them into his pockets, and when he raised his head, the old man was looking up into his face. He backed away, startled. The fellow said a few words, all the while beckoning.

Buddy shrugged his shoulders, then shook his head.

The man continued to squat there jabbering at him.

It was growing late. Buddy glanced up and down the street, wondering what he, Buddy Hilder, was doing in such a place. What business could he have here? He looked up at the sky. The stars were gone. A dark damp film wrapped the village as if a poisonous cloud had settled on the world.

"I got to be going," Buddy said to the old man.

He looked again at the silhouettes scattered on the ground. The old man repeated his words over and over. He thrust out his hand, drew it back, thrust it out again. Of a sudden, Buddy saw, between the yellow fingers, his own likeness: his forehead, nose and chin, done in black paper. He turned quickly away.

The snow fell more heavily. As Buddy made his way back to join the others, he looked over his shoulder in time to see his silhouette, loosed from the old man's fingers, drop, fluttering, down to join the rest.

A Well of Living Water

4.

Nose Jaccaud never looked warm again after the night he was thrown into the shower with his clothes on. He went around blowing on his hands with his shoulders hunched over his hollow chest.

And though Buddy could tell Nose was trying his best to act on his advice and let on he didn't care when the fellows short-sheeted his bed, tied knots in his clothes, poured syrup into his shoes and painted his toenails while he slept, his big eyes grew ever more aggrieved and doleful.

One evening, as Buddy lay reading on his bunk in the nearly empty barracks, he looked up to see Newell, Johnson and O'Malley row in crocked as moonshiners. They sat down on Newell's bunk and made a stab at playing blackjack with a great deal of swearing and slapping down of cards.

When they finished playing, Big Dick Johnson went into the latrine and was sick. O'Malley and Newell came down and sat on Jaccaud's bunk.

"Where's Nose?" O'Malley inquired, frowning. He looked under the bed.

"Yes. Where in hell is the sadsack bastard?" Newell asked, moving his long upper lip exaggeratedly at each syllable. "We want to teach him strip poker."

"Caught guard duty," Buddy told them.

"Jesus! If a gook came at Nose, he'd shit his pants," O'Malley opined. "He'd hand the camp over quicker than spit."

"Hilder wouldn't!" Newell crowed, thumping Buddy's back. "He'd do his duty and shoot the little mother-fucker.

'Hilder don't drink nor cuss nor chew,
  He don't go with girls who do.'

"What you reading, Hilder, the Bible?"

"A book on sheep."

"Sheep! Whatever the hell for?"

"When I leave the army, I plan on raising sheep."

"A kid I knew said he fucked a sheep," O'Malley observed gravely. "Say, Hild, is that possible?"

"Don't be asking Hilder such a question!" Newell remonstrated. "You'll shock him out of his socks!"

"What in Chrissname may this be?" O'Malley asked from where he leaned against the windowsill.

"That's Nose's truck garden," said Newell.

A Well of Living Water

"The hell you say."

"Next week he's fixing to hang lace curtains on the window."

Big Dick walked up behind them, looking pale and cross. He gave Buddy a shove that shook up his lights and liver as he reached over his shoulder to collar O'Malley.

"You owe me four bucks eighty," he said.

"Wait until I get done admiring this posy," O'Malley told him.

"It ain't a posy. It's a goddamn bean," Newell put in.

Big Dick stumped around to stare into the pot. "Whatever it is," he said, "it needs watering." He took a can of lighter fluid out of his shirt pocket.

Buddy came up onto his knees, opened his mouth to object, thought better of it and, closing his mouth, watched silently while Johnson poured the fluid into the pot.

Johnson replaced the can in his pocket. "Gimme my four bucks eighty," he said and fetched O'Malley a one-handed clout that sent him sprawling over Nose's bed. They scuffled and rolled onto the floor.

When Buddy went to the bean plant, lifted the pot and peered in, the lighter fluid had already sunk into the dirt.

Buddy was alone in the barracks when Nose came off guard duty. He watched the bony youth slouch wearily up the aisle. A damp outdoors smell hung onto his clothes. He shrugged himself out of his coat and kicked off his boots. His sorrowful eyes looked enormous in his blue, pinched face.

"Wrap a blanket around you," Buddy advised him. "You're shaking the whole room."

"It was pissing cold along the tracks. Where is everybody?"

"Over at the beer hall. Or taking in the movie."

"Well, it's quiet, ain't it?"

Nose walked to the window ledge and looked at the bean plant. He stood in front of it for a long time. Then he picked up the pot in both hands and sniffed.

Buddy moved his shoulders uneasily.

Nose turned around and looked at Buddy. "Was it you done it?" he asked.

Buddy shook his head.

Nose sat down on his bunk with the bean plant on his knees. For a long while, there was silence. Outside, a group of soldiers passed, singing. Buddy tried to go on with his book. Now and again he glanced over at Nose, whose eyes had become somewhat vacant.

By the time the other men began to come back into the barracks, laughing and talking, thumping their boots across the bare floor, Nose's shoulders had taken on

A Well of Living Water

a rigid look.

The din in the barracks subsided. Buddy got under his blankets. The hour grew late. Long after the lights were put out, Buddy could yet see Nose sitting silhouetted against the pale square of the window. At last Nose, too, undressed and crawled into his bunk.

At about two o'clock, a high-pitched wailing brought the men up onto their feet, clawing the air.

"What issat? Air raid siren?"

"No. It's something alive. It's a animal."

"A wolf outside the windows."

"No. It's in here with us. It's down that way."

"Let's have some light, then."

Buddy was the first to see Nose Jaccaud lying on the floor beside his bed, rolling his head from side to side, twisting his mouth, biting his lips as he gave out the eerie wailing sound.

"Nose's having a fit!" Newell cried out. "Get the medic over here before he chews up the goddamn barracks."

5.

The end of the next week, at mail call, Buddy got a black-edged letter. It was from his Aunt Lou Fowler. His hands shook as he tore it open.

"Buddy," it read, "yore gramma is laid down beside yore grampa and yore mama in Conor's Bluff Cemetery. It was her heart stopped on her. She'd knowed since before you left as her days was numbered. She died in the Lord and is gone to glory. Amen. Come visit me, Buddy, when yore soldiering is done."

Buddy kept his sorrowing to himself. As the weeks passed, he was grateful for the long hard hours of work. Because of them, his grief fell from him more quickly.

Days he ran his shovel on the airstrip; nights he went to the movies on the base and so kept out of trouble. He had put in for his first pass to Tokyo, and he didn't want anything to keep it from coming through.

All went well, until late one afternoon he realized he'd forgotten to make a fuel pick-up.

He was pacing up and down in front of his helper's truck, stopping to slap the hood now and then, when Newell passed by.

"Hey, Hild! Time to knock off, partner," Newell cried out.

"I got to get gas fer them cats and shovels," Buddy said. "Where's my gook? I want him to drive me to the fuel dump."

"You was supposed to do that this morning. The sergeant'll have your skinny neck for sure, Hilder. Your gook's gone home."

"Ain't they a truck I can take?"

"Only that one, and you dassn't lay a finger on it account of your gook owns it. I'd stay and help you worry, only I got to write to my girl in Cleveland. Man oh man, am I ready to go state-side any time now. Did you hear they shipped old Jaccaud home? The lucky son-of-a-bitch! Turns out he's a goddamn epileptic."

Newell went his way. Buddy glanced impatiently over the base. Nothing to see but khaki britches and muddy boots. In the city, there would be colored lights and bands playing, and shops where he could buy his Aunt Lou Fowler a pair of silk pajamas.

Quicker than thought, Buddy opened the truck's hood and hot-wired the ignition. Every part of the engine was spotlessly clean, oiled, perfectly tuned. The motor purred at once. He climbed behind the wheel. The inside of the cab had been scrubbed and brushed. Each window shone.

At the fuel dump, Buddy directed the loading of the barrels. Sliding back under the wheel, he saw that the sun had dipped low. If he didn't look out, he'd be late for chow and get in dutch yet.

He sent the truck leaping back down the narrow road. He was halfway to the base when he spotted an army jeep coming toward him and realized too late that he was driving down the wrong side of the highway.

He hit the brake. Swerving, he managed to miss the jeep, but the truck dropped off the road and went out of control. He plowed through a field and came to a jarring stop against a tree.

Buddy climbed out of the truck, shaking his head and feeling of his bones. He was unhurt, but the truck, a new army surplus model, was crumpled and bent. It had to be towed back to the base.

"You sure smashed hell out of that truck!" Newell said admiringly the next day when Buddy, on the way back to the barracks, paused to look it over outside the motorpool. "What detail you think you'll pull?"

"Lord knows!" Buddy said mournfully. "They done already cancelled my pass and docked my pay to fix the front end. Whatever they do to it, though, it ain't never going to be the same."

They had started on when, of a sudden, Newell glanced back over his right shoulder.

"What's that mother-fucker up to?" Newell asked.

"Where?"

"See him squatting there in front of the truck? It's a gook!"

"What's he doing?"

"I don't know. Sort of running his hand over the grille like he's feeling up a woman. Hey, boy!"

The Japanese straightened and stood, his back to them, facing the motorpool.

"What you want there?" Newell shouted shrilly, wagging his finger at the man.

"That's my gook!" said Buddy, suddenly recognizing the man. "Look here," he said, retracing his steps and taking hold of his helper's skinny shoulder. "I'm right sorry I wrecked yore truck."

The man swiveled his head to look at Buddy. His mouth worked, but he didn't speak. As Buddy and Newell watched, still silent, he walked away across the airstrip, his shrunken shadow following at his heels like a black, misshapen child.

"Did you see the face he was making?" Newell marveled. "He looked like Jaccaud having his fit."

"He looked like Gramma Wheat," said Buddy, "the day I joined the army."

"How in the hell," Newell wanted to know, "can a gook look like your grandmother?"

All that evening, Buddy sat on his bunk staring at an open book without turning the pages.

Just before the men started to come in, he rolled over and closed his eyes. After the lights went out, he opened them again.

An hour passed. Then another. The men lay along the walls, each motionless on his own bunk. During the third hour, the moon rose.

As it climbed the sky, its light streaked the ceiling, leaving the floor shadowed so that Buddy had the sensation of lying deep down in darkness while, over his head, yellow flowers bloomed.

A Well of Living Water

BOOK II MARGARET

Part I Twister

1.

The piquant child leaned out the door calling, "Come, Gibbet, come!"

The woman, tall and broad of shoulder, turned from her loom to watch the child, a shadow settling in her clear eyes.

"The cat won't come, Margaret," she said.

"Why not?"

"She's gone away."

"Where?"

"Away. Step outdoors and tell me: is it going to rain? What do you think?"

The woman watched good-humoredly while her child ran out into the yard and stared up at the sky.

"It ain't raining now."

"But it will, do you think?"

"No. It won't."

"Because you want it shouldn't?"

A Well of Living Water

"No. Because it won't. They's only a little cloud on the sun."

"Then we'll go."

Jane Geist passed the shuttle once more between the warp threads and laid it on top of the loom. Beneath, the yarns were twisted into a simple patterned fabric. The warp was white and the waft black. Jane had learnt the craft of her granny. She made a few blankets and rugs now and again for what money they brought and for the pleasure of the work. She stood up, stretching her strong arms.

"Fetch my jacket, Ma."

"Yes. And then we'll start."

Jane wrapped on her own shawl, handed the child her jacket, and stood waiting. The little girl held out her jacket and thrust her arm through the sleeve.

"No, that's wrong. You'll have it backwards."

Again the child put in her arm.

"No. Take the short side, Margaret."

Tears of vexation started in the little girl's eyes.

"You help, Ma."

Jane took the jacket and with a respectful air held it while her daughter stuck in one arm and then the other.

"Now we're ready," she said, taking up her husband's lunch pail from the table.

The two passed out of the house and over the lot by the barn, and so into the woods. For several yards through the woods, Margaret went along looking under the bushes and behind the trees calling, "Come, Gibbet. Come, Gibbet."

At last, seeming to grow tired of the vain search, she squatted down by a sumac bush watching a spider strap the leaves one to another in an intricate design.

"Now that's a present for you," Jane said seriously as the wind fluttered the web. "A glad sight on a dark day."

"See," said Margaret.

"Yes. But I can't get so close," Jane laughed, continuing on her way. "I can't squinch down like you."

"Why not?"

"Because you are four and I'm forty-five and my back hurts me. You're the child of my old age, Margaret. You've got to be patient."

Margaret ran here and there amongst the trees. Now and again the sun, as it dipped in and out of the clouds, caught in the fine yellow mist of her hair.

What a tiny mite she was, and how intense! Her mother followed after her, amused, marveling. After so many years, to have such a child! Jane's being thawed and lightened at the sight of her. Marking Margaret running ahead, she surely beheld a bright living piece of her own soul moving free. She continued on dreamily.

"Look here," she said suddenly, bending down and plucking a leaf. "Put this in your mouth and chew it."

"It's tea," said the child, tasting.

"Well then, you're a smart cookie because you're right. It's sassafras. I used to chew it in the woods when I was little. On the way back, we'll dig some roots."

"Do this, Ma," Margaret cried, suddenly grabbing her mother's hand and laying one large blunt finger on her own forehead.

"But we must hurry to Pa."

"No. Do this."

"Pa's been plowing since daybreak. You and me's got to fetch him his pail. He's hungry."

"Do this."

"All right." Jane looked into her daughter's serious bright little face and began pointing out her features slowly, one by one. "Forehead backer, eye winker, tom tinker, nose dropper, mouth eater, chin chopper."

Here Margaret began to squeal and scream and to tuck down her chin against the tickling "Gulley, gulley, gulley!" which came anyway.

"Do it again."

Jane kissed her daughter solemnly on the vein in the warm inside bend of her arm.

"No. Run on."

'I spoil her,' the mother thought wistfully. 'I keep her by me and pet her and talk to her minute by minute. But she lifts me so.'

"Listen to this," she called to Margaret, and she raised her hands and, cupping them, blew upon her thumbs, sending forth a low penetrating whistle.

"Now, hark."

Mother and daughter stood quite motionless, listening. Soon an answering whistle came from far away through the trees.

"That was your pa," Jane said, nodding. "Now he knows we're coming."

"I want to blow."

"You're too small to make a peep. Well, then, you see, you must hold your hands so. No, palm to palm. Bend your thumbs."

Margaret grew very red in the face from blowing the breath through her hands.

"I can't."

"Keep trying. It'll come."

"No. I can't."

A Well of Living Water

The child stamped her foot and blew and blew.

"Try this then," said the mother, amused and patient, but pitying her. She reached out with her strong arms and lifted Margaret up to the top branches of a young sapling.

"Now catch hold the top there. Grip on tight."

Jane let the child go so that she swung out, her thin legs kicking free in the air. Slowly, the limber trunk bowed lower and yet lower, until its leafy top branches touched the ground, rustling. Margaret found her footing and let go of the tree and it sprang back into the air, quivering.

"Do it again."

"No. Now we've got to get on. My dad licked me for bending down the trees."

"Did you play with the trees, Ma, when you was little like me?"

"Yes. And I dammed up the creek and waded. I picked wildflowers and stood them in jars. I found fairy rings where the toadstools grow in a circle. I made cups and saucers out of acorns. We'll fetch some home and I'll show you. The woods is full of playthings. Or you can work and sing and dance all yourself, and that's a-plenty to fill your days."

The trees began to thin out as Jane and Margaret approached the field. Margaret went and stood by a sapling, excitedly feeling at the bark, crying, "Make a whistle, Ma."

Jane laughed out, throwing back her broad shoulders.

"You know what a willow is, but I ain't got a knife this trip. Look here where the trees is scarce. There's sweet william and here's spring beauties blooming and bloodroot. Look for a trillium, but don't pull it off else it'll wither."

Margaret dropped to her knees and began to search under the leaves while her mother continued on to the field. Jane went with her heart yearning backward to the little one. What a spark of life she was, with her quick thin little body and her cloud of fine hair. How nimbly she doubled up, squatting amongst the fragile woods posies.

Of a sudden, Jane ached with an extremity of love as swollen in her as a milk-full breast yet unsucked. The child and the flowers roused her so. She looked back from the edge of the field and saw them nestled in the dappling shadow under the branches.

Her husband walked behind the horses, the leather lines tied behind his hips, guiding the plow with his familiar, weathered hands around the hill field which rose too steep for the use of a tractor.

"Bob," she called, and he left the plow and came to her stepping wide across the turned earth, while behind him the horses rested in the traces with their heads down. She handed him the pail.

"Where's Margaret?"

"At the edge of the woods there."

"The wind's uncommon strong."

"Yes."

"Bet and Dolly is skittish. There's maybe a storm coming."

"I don't think so."

"Well."

"You're tired, old man," she said tenderly. His shirt was black with sweat over his bony shoulders, and his mouth lay lax where the tobacco juice stained the corners.

"Yes, old woman," he said, smiling a little but straightening himself and strong enough still and content.

"Now then, I'll take the horses around while you eat."

"There's no need."

"I like to do it. If you finish by sundown, you can plant tomorrow as you've been fretting to do."

"Yes."

He sat on a stump and ate, watching his wife follow the horses around the field. The wind pressed her dress to her long thighs. He saw her shoulders strong and heavy as she pulled back on the lines. Her eyes were on the point of the plow where it parted the furrow. She came round to him once and yet again.

"Jane."

"Yes."

"Now give the horses a drink and let them rest."

She unhitched them from the plow and led the great heavy beasts to the spring down the field's edge. She let them blow, tethered there.

"Listen at this, Jane."

"Why, what's the matter?"

"Hark over yonder in the trees."

Man and wife stood still, listening. Margaret's voice came to them, carried piping and frail on the wind.

"Here, Gibbet. Here, Gibbet."

"Well," said Jane, troubled but not owning it. "And so she calls the cat."

"You had ought to tell her it's dead, Jane."

"No."

"Yes. You know you had ought."

"She'd only grieve her soul over it."

A Well of Living Water

"And so she should."

"Still, I pity her."

"You can't keep her from death, Jane."

"I can for a little."

"She should know young that the wild dogs will gut a kitten. It's a natural end."

"It's a shame, too."

Bob looked at his wife. Her face was flushed with the plowing. Perspiration stood on her lip and he shook his head and laughed at her.

"You're a lively woman, Jane," he said.

Weak and foolish with the pleasure of the food in his belly and the relief of resting his body after the long morning's labor, he delighted in her and how her concern was all with life. There was no room for death in her.

"I am, yes," she answered him calmly.

"You can out-plow any man that lives."

"Yes."

"But you shelter Margaret too much. You do too much for her. You don't let her learn to do for herself, for you and for other folks as well. You must let her alone to sorrow or laugh as it comes to her. You protect her overly, I think, Jane. You teach her about life but you hide away death."

"She should know both, as they're threads of the same cloth. She must learn to live with dying all around her, you know. That's how we all must learn to live."

"Why, yes," Jane said, weary of the talk. "I'll tell her about the cat, then."

Satisfied, Bob went to hitch the horses once more to the plow. As Jane turned from him, she saw Margaret coming out of the woods, her short skirts held to her waist and filled with wild blossoms. The wind swept her along and lifted her hair like a bit of fluff.

"See, Ma?" she piped gladly.

"I see. Come down to the spring, Margaret, and we'll soak the stems and wrap them in wet leaves so they won't fade," Jane said.

They went along the edge of the field together, stepping where the warm earth was turned up to the sun waiting to receive the seed.

Then, the flowers cool and dripping, mother and daughter took their way slowly home through the darkening wind-whipped forest, stopping to pull up sassafras roots along the path, and to gather acorns amongst last fall's leaves.

Dusk fell early, and the family ate supper with the lamps lit. Afterward, Bob smoked his pipe on the porch, watching the clouded western sky which remained red long after the sun had set.

2.

Late that night, Margaret awoke to find that the light in the hall was not burning. She sat up, wide awake, and called out, but no one came. It was strangely close and hot.

Sweat trickled down the child's neck from under the short fine cloud of her hair.

"Ma."

No one answered.

And "Ma, Ma," the child called again, kicking her thin short legs over the edge of the bed and sliding to the floor in the dark.

Through the open window she could see the wind behaving like an angry puppy, tearing at the trees. She could hear it worrying the walls of the house until they groaned again.

Margaret padded up to the window. Lightning flashed unnaturally in an intermittent brightness, as if someone were switching a light quickly on and off and yet again on. She saw that the sky was glowing in colors behind the clouds.

"Pa."

She went down the stairs, and her parents were nowhere. The wind banged and shouted.

"Ma, Ma," she said, and opened the door and went out into the yard. Margaret was rather frail and small of frame. The wind nearly sucked her up. The limb of a tree twice the size of her leg tumbled past her left ear and went bouncing off across the barn lot.

Intent of purpose, she continued on to the barn. Her face was expressionless and absorbed, like a small fetus. She was outraged that her parents did not come. She was awestruck by her own fear at their absence, which was very great.

She found that she could not open the barn door. As she stood tugging at it, silent and numb, overwhelmed by the strangeness of being out-of-doors at night, a spider dropped suddenly from the door onto her arm, crept over her hand and away. Then, although it was May, hail began to rattle on the ground. Bouncing up, it stung the child's bare ankles.

Margaret saw it plainly in the lightning flashes which came always closer together. She watched, all at once delighted, as the small white balls jumped about at her feet.

She started when the wind fairly shook the barn from side to side and up and down. There was the sound of a deep-throated roaring. She listened open-mouthed. The wind roared exactly like a train.

A Well of Living Water

"Ma!"

Margaret worked at the handle on the barn door, and suddenly the entire door pulled from her and went sailing off loose and free, spinning around and around up over her head and away. The air was filled with flying boards and shingles from the walls and roof of the barn.

The heavy-handed wind passed away quickly, and rain began to fall.

Margaret stood blinking, looking with a puzzled expression at the space where the barn had been. When the rain had wet her through, she was cold and she began to cry. It took her a long time to return to the house, since a tree had been uprooted between the house and barn, and she must crawl through the dripping branches.

It was useless effort since the house, too, was gone. Only the cellar remained, yawning darkly at her feet.

Two men from Trent, Doctor Joe Bryant and the fire chief, Fred Kimes, found her there in the morning, sitting quietly in her nightdress on the edge of the cellar with her small hands folded in her lap.

They spoke to her gently. They wished to question her, but she paid them no mind. They could not catch her eye. Instead, she looked off toward the woods.

They turned away from her to stare about. Debris covered the grass: broken two-by-fours, shards of roofing, a splintered table. A frying pan was lodged in the crotch of a tree. A piece of the loom lay tangled in the uprooted tree's branches, a few threads of the warp yarn still hanging to the frame.

Kimes lowered himself into the cellar.

"They're down here," he said almost at once.

"My God! I can see them," the doctor murmured. He leant forward, his thick white hair falling over his forehead. "I can see them from here."

"They're both down here and they're both dead," Chief Kimes went on wonderingly. "The woman is lying over the man like she was trying to shield him. There's kerosene all across the floor under these boards and a busted lantern.

"They never knew what hit the place. They was trying to fill the lantern when the house blew in on top of them."

"Then why is the little girl alive? There ain't a mark on her."

"She wasn't in the house," said Kimes. "She couldn't have been and lived. She must have been outside, some way or other."

"Ain't that odd!"

"It is. But then you know yourself the funnel was odd, the way it skipped over the village except for the west edge, and only took off a few roofs there."

Before removing the bodies from the cellar, the two men picked up the small girl and carried her to their car, where they placed her on the seat doubled up in a blanket.

"Now who'll raise her?" Chief Kimes asked. "She's got no kin I've heard about."

"God knows," said the doctor.

When they had finished and returned to the car, they found the child had not moved. She still crouched, blanket-wrapped as they had left her. Only the ends of her yellow hair lifted and fell on her shoulders, stirred by the morning breeze.

A Well of Living Water

Part II   Erdine

1.

At first Margaret hid in corners. Sitting in corners, she forgot how to button and how to eat with a fork.

"She ain't used to being with other children, you see," the matron told the cook. "Her parents was old and lived in the country. Besides, she got the lion's share, poor thing. They doted on her."

As the weeks in the Kimball County Children's Home came and went, then the months and the years, Margaret gradually took up the care of her small body once more.

She moved about the rooms washing her face, eating her food, making her bed and mending her clothes. But when she had time to herself, she still hunted corners where she curled up with her books or her thoughts. Tightly-squeezed and dim and safe, the corners seemed to Margaret. There was no wind in them.

"What are you sitting there for, Margaret?" the matron would call. "What are you hiding from?"

"I ain't hiding," Margaret said as the matron took her arm.

"What is it you are doing then?"

"I'm looking at the beds."

"The point is you are to get into one of them."

"They's too many beds all alike."

"I'll tell the Board your opinion," said the matron with amiable sarcasm, chuckling to herself. She pulled the girl's nightdress down over her head.

"And all of them children in the beds..."

"Well, what about them?"

"They come and they go away," Margaret said, "and they ain't got no faces, only the backs of their heads laying on the pillows."

"If you'd stop hiding in corners, you'd see their faces."

"I think they ain't got no faces."

"Then you're a silly goose."

"I think their faces ain't there at all."

After Matron went her way, Margaret lay awake, staring at the rows of beds, and she knew she was right, for not one child turned its face toward her.

It was dark in the orphanage building, even when the sun was shining. The windows were small and high up. The yard outside was dust or mud, according to the weather. On one side was a pump, on the other a cistern with a rotting wooden top. The fence around the yard was made of criss-crossed wire. A few wilted blades of grass grew by the posts of the gate. Beyond the fence were the houses of the village of Trent.

When Margaret was nine, Erdine Lincoln returned to the orphanage. She stepped up the front walk like royalty coming home.

"Here, kiddie!" she said to a pale small girl named Penny Brock, sliding her suitcase handle graciously into the child's thin hands. "Ain't you glad I'm back?"

"Yes," said Penny, and the two girls went around together afterward.

It was Penny crying several weeks later that brought Margaret out of the corners.

"What're you bawling for?" Margaret asked curiously, after she had stood for a while in wonder watching the tears roll down Penny's face and drop off her chin into her lap, where she was twisting her hands together.

"None of your beeswax," said Penny.

She had two brown braids and was narrow as a willow shoot.

"You're making an awful racket," said Margaret, and she stuck her fingers into her ears.

"You just wait till *your* best friend don't like you no more," said Penny. "Then see what kind of racket you make, smarty pants."

The next day when Margaret came into the sleeping room, she found Penny

A Well of Living Water

and Erdine quarreling.

"Look here, kiddie, you only brought one of my shoes. Where's the other?" Erdine exclaimed impatiently.

"I don't know."

"But I got to have it. I sent you out to fetch both. What good will one do me, you ninny?"

"I looked all around the bush where you said."

"Well, go look again."

"I can't go back now. It's my night to set table."

"Go set it then, but you'll be sorry," Erdine said with an ugly look.

Penny, her big eyes teary, went to the dining room.

"Come in, kiddie," called Erdine to Margaret, smoothing her black shingled hair. "You can't imagine how I been wanting to talk to you. You think I ain't noticed you? Say, I've seen you around. I even said to Matron, 'Who is that cute little girl with the curly hair?' You can ask her if I didn't. Them's my exact words. What's your name?"

"Margaret."

"I was fooling you. I knew your name, but I wanted to hear you say it. I'm Erdine. Is your parents both dead?"

"Yes."

"You're lucky, kiddie," Erdine went on, biting at her cuticles. "My old lady is still breathing and I wish to hell she wasn't. Every time she gets married she boots me out, and here I am again."

"Has she been married much?"

"My lord I think so! Yes."

"Did you know Penny before?"

"Yes. Bad Penny, I call her. God how she turns up and turns up. I don't care much for her. She thinks I do, but I don't."

"Why not?"

"She's such a stupid little nubbin. And she's got a bad heart. She's always sick. I can't stand sick people, can you? But here's the secret: Penny has this great-aunt that gives her presents. Last week she sent her a jointed doll with a tin head. Even its knees bend! Next spring she's going to bring her a kitten. This aunt always sends her candy and toys. That's the reason I keep her around. She's so dumb she gives it all away."

Erdine laughed in an unpleasant way, her bony shoulders heaving, her freckles standing out darkly on her white skin.

"Do you want some scent?" she asked suddenly throwing open her suitcase

A Well of Living Water

upon the bed. Her movements were quick and intense as she looked round with her shiny dark eyes like a bird or a rat uncovering its nest.

"All right," said Margaret, stepping closer.

"Lean down. I'll spray you. Hold your nose or it'll make you sneeze."

There was a quick whispered sigh and the air smelt heavily of musk.

"Mmmm. Ain't that nice?"

"Yes."

"Don't you love it?"

"Yes."

"Oh, kiddie, it's superb. But then I knew you'd say so."

"Why?"

"Because I can tell about people. It's a gift I got, this telling what people is like. I knowed you was smart as soon as I seen you. I said to Penny, 'There's a smart kid.' You ask her if I didn't. She'll tell you. Them's my exact words."

"Will you stay long this time?"

"The good Lord knows, kiddie. I want to, now you're here."

"Why?"

"You know it's because I like you. You got good taste. You know nice items when you see them. Like my scent and your ring there. Lemme see that."

Margaret started when the older girl took hold of her hand. Erdine's fingers were moist, long and limber, uncommonly vibrant and alive. Margaret shivered at her touch.

"That's silver, ain't it? That's superb. Where'd you get that?"

"Doctor Joe brought it to me. He comes to see me sometimes."

"I like it. Sit by me at supper."

"We got to sit where they tell us."

"You think I don't know that? Say, I grew up here, kiddie. But you can sit by me if I say so. It'll be all right."

"I will, then."

The dinner bell rang and they went down together.

"I've been waiting for you," Erdine cried excitedly one afternoon as Margaret came out into the yard after lunch. "Come sit on the fence. This'll be our special place."

"All right."

"Bad Penny's in the infirmary and I'm a little bit glad because I want to read this to you, kiddie, by yourself. It's a story I'm inventing. I'll publish it later. It's

A Well of Living Water

superb."

"You mean you're making it up out of your own head?"

"Yes. I make up stories all the time. I just do it like other people breathe. It's a gift I got."

"What's it about?"

"It's about a girl who's real poor. Nobody will talk to her because she's so ragged but her mother turns out to be a movie star and her father is a king with a army and scads of precious jewels and the girl tells her father's army to kill the people who was mean to her and she and her parents ride away in their gold Cadillac car in the end. Only there's a deal more to it."

Margaret listened marveling while Erdine read out loud for the better part of an hour. She listened to other stories on many days thereafter.

"We're such good friends," Erdine called over one night as they lay in bed. "We'll adore one another forever, won't we?"

"Yes," said Margaret.

"No matter where we go, we'll always remember. Here's what we must do, kiddie." Erdine suddenly sat up in bed. "Have you got a pin?"

"No."

"Shh. Don't wake up those other sillies. Here. I've got my pajama top pinned together in front where the button came off."

"Have you got the button? I'll sew it on for you tomorrow."

"All right. Now stretch out your arm."

Margaret felt Erdine's fingers lay hold of her hand and turn up the palm so that the veined underside of her arm shone white. She felt a sharp pain as Erdine jabbed in the pin. A tiny plume of dark blood jetted up and spread.

Erdine sat watching Margaret's arm, a deep shadow over her face. Then quickly she touched her own arm with the pin and pressed the two arms, hers and Margaret's, together.

"Your arm is so warm," Margaret said wonderingly, trembling.

"Now we're sisters, kiddie," Erdine whispered, her laughter coming in an uncontrolled gasp that was almost hysterical. "We got each other's blood in us forever."

She took her arm away, and Margaret almost wept to feel it gone and her own arm cold and exposed with the blood crusting on it.

"Have you got a dollar bill?" Erdine asked.

"Yes, I have. Hid in the bottom of my clothes drawer. Doctor Joe give it to me last Christmas."

A Well of Living Water

"Fetch it here and I'll show you something. I'd use my money, but I ain't got no bills. Now watch this."

Margaret attended, awestruck, as Erdine carefully folded the dollar precisely in half and tore it down the crease. She handed half the bill back to Margaret and kept the other half in her fingers.

"Now," she whispered, "wherever we may go in this whole world and no matter how we're changed, when we meet again we must match the halves of this bill and we'll know we're true friends and blood sisters. Ain't that superb? I read that in a book."

Margaret lay awake into the night, her throbbing arm wrapped in the bed covers, watching Erdine's sleeping face.

2.

On Valentine's Day, a new girl came to the Home. She was an elegant child with natural blond curls. She owned many dresses, and the silk stockings she wore kindled wonder in every child who saw them. She also had a father who visited her on Sundays.

Margaret, of all the children, took little notice of her, absorbed as she was with Erdine.

The children played at fox and geese in the snow. Erdine and Margaret, when they were geese together, ran until they gasped all around and around the outer path of the circle. Sometimes Erdine was the fox and Margaret, hid among the other geese, watched the tall bony figure creeping quickly along the paths.

The other geese ran squealing away around the wheel and only Margaret stayed behind, too rapt to move, and was caught.

Toward the end of February, Erdine turned moody. The freckles stood out darkly on her pale cheeks, and she scarcely spoke a word to Margaret all day long. At night she turned her face away.

One lunchtime, Margaret bent her head with its mist of fine hair close to Erdine's as she sat down in her place, murmuring,

"You ain't mad at me, are you?"

"No."

"You act like you are."

"When I don't talk, it means I'm thinking," Erdine said loftily. "It means I'm studying on certain items. I got a right to study things out, haven't I?"

A Well of Living Water

"Yes."

"Well, don't pick at me, then."

"I'm not."

"Well, then, just leave me be a while. Why do you have to stand around staring at me all the time?"

"But I don't."

"Yes, you do. Just like a silly idiot. I saw you watching me have a private conversation with that new girl Bonnie Frey. You just forever stand breathing down my neck and eyeing me."

"I wanted to give you something, but you never looked around."

"What?"

"Reach your hand here. Open your fingers. There. Now close them."

"Your ring? Oh kiddie, you shouldn't give me your ring. What will your friend say? He'll make you get it back."

"He won't notice. If he does, I'll say it pinched me and I put it away."

"Ain't it superb?" cried Erdine. "Look at how it just fits me."

Early in March, Penny's great-aunt brought her a small striped kitten. One afternoon, finding it on the window ledge outside the dining room, Erdine raised the window and lifted the kitten in out of the snow.

"It ain't allowed in," Penny whispered, alarmed.

"Who'll know but you and me and Margaret? We're all that's here and we ain't going to tell."

"Somebody might come in."

"Don't be such a 'fraidy calf. You're always afraid."

"I'm not."

"You're afraid to sneeze or blow your nose or go to the john for fear you'll get caught in the wrong."

"What are you doing?"

"I'm going to fix this pussy a set of paper stockings. Hold it like this, on its back."

"What for?"

"You just watch. My mom used to do this to our cats at home and we died laughing at them."

"It's trying to scratch you."

"If it does, it'll wish it hadn't. Now let go."

The cat, finding itself suddenly free, sniffed in alarm at the four small rolls of paper encasing its legs. It shook one hind leg, then the other, but the paper, fastened in place with rubberbands, remained. The kitten walked a few steps, twitched its front feet and began to back across the floor slowly, continuing to shake its feet one at a time.

Erdine laughed until the tears stood in her eyes.

"Look, kiddie," she cried to Margaret. "Look!"

The kitten, now thoroughly frightened, leaped straight up into the air, stiff-legged, once, twice, then a third time.

"Take them off, Erdine," Penny said. She began to whimper.

Now the kitten raced about the room bumping into the chairs and table legs, wringing its feet as it ran. Margaret could see the wind whirling snow outside, while inside the small animal flew in and out of the corners.

"Oh, the poor thing," Penny cried, hugging her elbows to her thin body.

The door to the dining room slammed open and a crowd of children stood staring in. At the front the new girl, Bonnie Frey, with her silk hose on, gaped to see the cat now jumping high in the middle of the room.

Still kneeling, Erdine bent her face and her bony shoulders toward the door. The short black hair stood out at the nape of her neck as she and Bonnie Frey fixed one another with their eyes.

The kitten, having managed to free itself of all but one of the rolls of paper, whisked out at the door and down the hall. The children turned and ran after it, shouting.

At night when they lay in their beds side by side, Erdine began to talk to Margaret about the new girl, Bonnie.

"Kiddie, she's so stuck up," she whispered, lying on her side, facing Margaret in the darkness. "She thinks she's so swell, you know. Doesn't she think she's swell?"

"Yes."

"She won't even speak. She holds her nose in the air and won't even say 'hello.' She passed me twice in the hall this morning and never even as much as nodded."

Margaret hardly attended to Erdine's words. She lay listening sleepily to the murmur of Erdine's voice coming to her ears across the darkness.

"She thinks she's so big because her father brings her presents every Sunday."

"Does he?"

"Yes. Last Sunday he gave her a watch. A real one. It was a cheap one, though."

"Is he rich?"

"He must be, kiddie. He drives this superb car. A maroon Buick sedan. He's

A Well of Living Water

going to take her away as soon as the court settles he can have her. Her mother's trying to get her, too."

In the moonlight reflected from the snow, Margaret could trace the shape of Erdine's face strained toward her above the sheets. She fell asleep while she gazed at it.

In a week's time, whenever Margaret looked for Erdine, she found her walking with Bonnie. Day after day it was always the same.

In the corner of the yard, in a room of the house, she came upon the black head and the yellow head bent close together. When Margaret tried to join them, Erdine was sullen and angry until she moved on.

At bedtime one night, Margaret followed Erdine into the sleeping room and watched silently while Erdine gathered up her belongings from under the bed and then began to roll up her blankets.

"Bad Penny's in the infirmary again," Erdine remarked at last, panting from her labors. "So I'm switching beds with her. Hers is over beside Bonnie's. Look what Bonnie gimme to come sleep by her."

Erdine stuck out her arm. A small, rather tarnished watch was strapped around the wrist.

"It's Bonnie's old watch, kiddie. The one she had before her dad give her the white gold one. It don't run, but the jeweler said he'd fix it for a dollar."

"But don't move, Erdine. We can't talk no more if you move. I can't listen to your stories."

"I know, kiddie. I don't want to, but it's such a superb watch. I had to say I'd do it. I'll fool her though. I won't stay but a night and then I'll move back. You'll see."

But the nights stretched on and Erdine did not come back. Penny returned and slept in the bed beside Margaret.

It was several weeks before Margaret discovered the torn half of the dollar bill had been taken out of the bottom of her clothes drawer. She went in the evening to where Erdine and Bonnie were sitting together on Erdine's bed with the lamp shining on their heads.

"My part of the dollar's gone out of my drawer," she said so loudly that several of the girls looked around.

"Of course it is, you stupid little nubbin," Erdine cackled, throwing back her bony shoulders. "I took it myself."

"What for?"

A Well of Living Water

"Why, to get this watch fixed, what do you think? I paid the jeweler with our dollar. I knew you'd want me to do it. Hear? It ticks now."

She lifted up her wrist. She and Bonnie grinned at one another evilly, tickled beyond words.

"But I thought we was supposed to keep them pieces forever."

"Did you?"

"To know each other by."

"I guess I'll know you without any old torn-up money," Erdine shouted with a snort of laughter. "You'll be skinny-legged and fuzzy-haired just like you are right this minute. And you can tell me because I'll be rich and beautiful."

Bonnie stared at Erdine and turned pink with strangled mirth, though she barely opened her lips in a smile.

"But we're sisters. You shouldn't have taken away my dollar because we're sisters."

"Did you believe that?"

"Yes."

"But that was a joke, kiddie," Erdine giggled. "What a silly sport you are. I just stuck your arm to watch it bleed. I never even pricked my arm at all. I simply let on."

"Give me back the dollar."

"I tell you it's gone. I spent it."

"But it was mine. My dollar. And you shouldn't have taken it because we're sisters."

"Ha, ha. You ain't no kin of mine, kiddie. Thank the Lord."

At first Margaret thought about Erdine a lot. She woke in the night, picturing Erdine's face with its dark freckles and her limber moist fingers.

When she slept again, her dreams were about Erdine. She saw herself lying on the bottom of a cold sea looking up at Erdine threshing on the surface. How Erdine beat the water with her arms, striving to stay afloat!

Margaret longed to join her, but a darkness spread itself between Margaret on the bottom and Erdine on the surface, widening and thickening until Margaret could see Erdine no longer.

When the darkness lifted, the water lightened slowly, as a windowpane clears of steam or frost and, little by little, one sees through. But Margaret always awoke before the final clearing.

A Well of Living Water

3.

In the early days of spring, the orphanage children ran about the yard until their legs ached. They played at baseball and kick-the-can, or at jacks on the rotting cistern top. They threw off their jackets, wiped the sweat from their eyes, and stood in line at the pump to drink their bellies full of the icy water.

Penny, who was too frail to run with the others, wandered about the yard collecting straw and leaves.

"She reminds me of a trillium," Margaret said to Erdine.

"A trillium, what's that?"

"It's a wildflower that dies if you pick it."

"She looks more like a mushroom," observed Bonnie, who was standing nearby.

"Her aunt moved to California and hardly sends her a stick of gum anymore," Erdine said. "I can't stand sick people, can you, kiddie?"

"No," said Bonnie. "Their breath is putrid."

"What's she got over there in the corner anyhow?"

"She's got that scrawny cat in a box."

"She's had it there all week," said Margaret. "She feeds it pieces of meat she saves off her plate at supper."

"Let's go see it," Erdine cried.

The three girls moved to where Penny squatted before an orange crate from which the cat looked up at them with wide green eyes.

"Look at that, a cat in a box!" exclaimed Erdine.

"Ugh," said Bonnie. "Don't it stink!"

"It wants fed. Feed it something, Penny."

Penny, looking at the others uneasily, opened her handkerchief and, taking out a piece of ground meat, dropped it into the kitten's mouth. She kept her chin pressed against her thin neck, casting her whole face downward. Her braids hung limply over her shoulder blades.

"Why, Penny, you shouldn't keep a cat shut up. It'll die," Erdine cried out, staring at the kitten with a strange excitement.

"I'll bet it's got lice," Bonnie said, recoiling from the box distastefully.

"Has it got lice, Penny? Let me see if it has."

Erdine undid the lid, flipped it back and picked up the kitten in her moist fingers, laughing. The kitten began to open and close its mouth, mewing loudly.

"Give it here," Penny said, following after the older girl.

A Well of Living Water

"I believe it has got lice. See for yourself," Erdine called, and with a swift motion of her bony shoulders dropped the kitten into Bonnie's hands. Bonnie examined it gingerly and when Penny approached her, returned it to Erdine.

The two older girls repeated the hand-off several times, moving about the yard. Their eyes sought one another's with a sly look.

Penny followed after now Erdine, now Bonnie, her thin face puzzled and alarmed.

"You give it here to me," she demanded.

"Is this kitten really yours, kiddie?" Erdine asked at last, pausing with the animal sprawled on her palm.

"Yes."

"Then you ought to give it to me."

"Why?"

"Because I'm your friend. I've always been your friend, haven't I?"

"Yes," Penny said, stopping confusedly, staring at the kitten.

"Well, you're supposed to give presents to your friends. Can I have it?"

"No."

"But I'm so good to you. I came to see you in the infirmary, didn't I? And I gave you some scent?"

"Yes."

"Well then, you should give me this cat."

"I want it."

"If you won't give it to me, give it to Bonnie. She's your friend, too. She'd like to have a cat," cried Erdine, dropping the furry creature into Bonnie's open hand.

"No."

"Then give it to me. Will you? Please? Pretty please?"

Penny stared at Erdine. "All right," she whispered at last.

"Then here's what I'll do with it since you gave it to me and it's mine," Erdine cried out in a transport of triumph, and she snatched the kitten from Bonnie and ran away across the yard with Penny, Bonnie and Margaret following after her. They saw Erdine run up to the cistern. She knelt, jerked up one of the weathered boards, and let the kitten drop inside.

The three girls stood gaping. Margaret moved closer and peered down into the dark hole.

"Why did you do that?" Bonnie cried out, loud with excitement.

"Because it was lousy," Erdine said, her voice choked.

The two older girls stared at one another over the cistern top. Bonnie watched Erdine's fingers, which had held the kitten, with an intense fascination.

A Well of Living Water

Penny, kneeling, gazed down into the cistern. She turned to Erdine, beginning to snuffle.

"Get it back," she said.

It was too much for Erdine and Bonnie. They ran away, whooping with laughter.

Margaret, however, stayed behind. She ripped a board from the cistern top, then another and another until she had made a hole large enough for her body to pass through. She let herself down into the cistern, hung for a moment at the rim taking a breath, then pushed herself under the water. She groped about until her lungs ached and her senses spun. Just when she had given the kitten up, her finger closed round it.

Rising with it through the dark water, she was conscious first of the bright sky, then of a dimness falling across her face, the shadow of Penny's head where she sat on a corner of the cistern, waiting.

BOOK III   THE WELLSPRING

1.

When Buddy came home from the army, he was afraid of the dark. There was no rhyme nor reason to the feeling, but as soon as the sun went down, his palms began to sweat and his nerves went all to hell. He got his medical discharge as much for that as for his ulcers.

Flying cross-country from San Francisco he was calm enough, as he was riding the train down into the hills. It was when a derailment made him get into Trent several minutes after midnight that he began to have trouble.

He stood in the station shaking in his shoes. Every soul on the train had thought himself a goner when the cars jumped the track. Buddy had helped pry an old woman out of the luggage rack.

He got a glass of milk to wash down his pills. Outside, he wished he'd drunk coffee because the wind had ice in it.

Trent was shut up tight. Buddy walked along the main drag with his suitcase bumping his knee, listening to the wind whistle through the empty streets. On the outskirts where his Gramma Wheat's house should have been, there was a Texaco station. He knew the place had gone for back taxes after she died, but he had

A Well of Living Water

expected the house to still be there. A high octane pump stood where his mama's jonquils had bloomed.

Out on the highway, it was like walking at the bottom of a well. The hills were all around him, timbered and inky black. Far overhead, a few pale stars shone.

There was no way out of the night except straight through it. Before he had taken a dozen steps, his stomach clenched and, in spite of the cold, sweat trickled down his back.

He knew Fowler's Mountain by its shape, somewhat like praying hands. At the top, the roof of his great-aunt's house peaked against the sky.

Going up the hill he climbed into a lighter world. The air freshened, and when he stopped and looked back, all the valley was featureless and dark below, like the ocean he had crossed and left behind.

The fields he'd come to till were there, though he couldn't see them. 'Buddy, why don't you come on home and mind the farm?' his Aunt Lou Fowler had written him. But not she herself. Since her stroke, she couldn't hold a pen. Not Garth, who was only six. But someone else who wrote a clear round hand that made the words look like ripe fruit. He wondered who.

Aunt Lou Fowler was asleep and his brother Garth was asleep. There were no lights. Above the house, thrust up against the stars, he saw the windmill. There it was, just as he remembered it, crouched on top of Fowler's Mountain, black and spidery as a giant daddy longlegs. He could already hear the creak of its blades turning in the cold wind.

Buddy wiped his sweating face on his sleeve. For years he'd thought he was a man, but that sound shut up time like a telescope and he was a kid again, afraid of Aunt Lou Fowler's windmill, scared it might suck the life out of him as if he were a fly.

Buddy went on up the hill, but instead of rousing them at the house, he let himself into the barn, climbed the ladder into the loft and flopped down on his back in the loose hay.

Because, Christ, he didn't want to be in a house. He didn't want to be that close to people. Not yet. People and the dark, that's what made his fucking stomach hurt. He covered his face with his hands and felt his fingers shaking where they lay across his eyes.

The air around him smelt of dried clover. The creak of the windmill was muffled in the barn. He heard sheep moving below him before he slept.

In the morning, a little snow fell. Buddy looked out of the loft and saw a girl sitting on the fence feeding a lamb from a bottle. She was a big strapping girl. Her shirt sleeves were rolled up above the elbows, and the hair on her arms shone golden. When he climbed down the ladder and looked for her, she was gone.

He went up to the house. His aunt was sitting in a rocker at the kitchen window and beckoned him in. She pulled him down, hugging him, so that his hat fell off and his face was squeezed against her breast. Garth stood in the corner drinking water out of a dipper, watching over the rim.

Buddy hadn't seen his Aunt Lou Fowler since her stroke. Her bright blue eyes were as he remembered them, and her silver hair and her smile. But he was shocked to see how heavily old age had come on her. She hadn't the use of one arm nor of her legs.

Oatmeal was set out on the table, and as he poured on the milk, he remembered the girl and looked through the window. There she was again, carrying two buckets up the hill. A pale plait hung down her back, but the short hairs around her face had pulled loose from the braid and made a mist that caught the morning sun. While he watched her, a large striped cat ran up the girl's back and sat perched on her shoulder washing itself. Buddy rubbed his eyes.

"Who is that outside?" he asked his aunt.

Garth came wiggling in between Buddy's knees and commenced playing with the buttons on his shirt.

"Aunt Lou can't talk," he said. "Outside, that's Margaret."

"Does she always have a cat on her back?"

"Yes. That's Gibbet. Margaret came from the orphanage. Margaret cooks supper and takes me walks in the woods and makes me willow whistles."

Buddy came to Fowler's Mountain at lambing season, and he didn't have time to take a good breath until April. He and Margaret delivered so many lambs he lost count. Then they docked and wormed the flock.

He got used to seeing Margaret with her shirt and arms spattered with blood and Gibbet sitting on her shoulder.

Margaret was a wonderful help to him. She was strong as any man he ever met. She worked by him long weary hours and never complained. She had a gentle way with the sheep so that they trusted themselves to her.

Nights, Buddy slept in the loft, and days, when he had the time and the sun was warm, he lay on the roof of the hog house, dozing. If Garth saw him, it was all up.

"Play catch, Buddy," he would scream, hooking his elbow over the fence and rocking back and forth. "Will you? Will you, Buddy?"

"Christ A'mighty!" said Buddy, swinging his legs over the edge of the hog house roof. "Stop bellering, can't you? You make my gut ache."

A Well of Living Water

"How come you stay in the pig lot all the time?"

"Because these pigs never pesters me to play ball. All they do is lay here and sleep and twitch off the flies with their ears."

"How's it going to hurt you to throw him a few?" Margaret said from where she stood under the windmill, washing clothes in a zinc tub.

"Hell!" said Buddy. He stood up on the roof of the hog house and held out his hands. Garth threw him the ball, shagging it over the fence.

"This is the poorest excuse for a ball I ever seen."

"It's the onliest one I got, though."

"This ball looks a million years old."

"It belongs to the drownded boys."

"The goddamn cover is coming off of it."

"Margaret can sew it."

Buddy followed the arc of the ball from his hand up into the air, down into Garth's hands. His eyes focused on Margaret standing beyond Garth, beating the clothes on the washboard, wringing them tight, shaking them out. The sun shone on her wet arms.

Beyond Margaret, in the kitchen window, his Aunt Lou Fowler sat looking out.

"Don't she give you the creeps?" Buddy said, suddenly lowering his voice and nodding his head toward the window. "Never talking?"

"She don't need to talk, Buddy," Margaret said. "You kin talk, and look what it's got you: stomach aches and nervous fits."

The ball sailed back and forth over the fence. Buddy scowled.

"Don't seeing her losing ground every day bother you?" he said.

But Margaret shook her head so her braid danced on her back.

"It just means she ain't got no time to fool away, Buddy," she said. "That's why she grabs us all the time like she does. It's hard for her to reach out, but every day she works at it, and every time she touches us, then she smiles. And oh, Buddy, I dearly love to see her smile!"

"That's because yo're all of you crazy up here on this mountain," Buddy said. He threw the ball so hard Garth dropped it and had to chase it. "You all got the same simple grin on yore faces, you and him and her. It's like you all belong to the same goddamn secret smiling society. And I'm blowed as I can see what you got to grin about.

"Here's you and Garth orphants and Aunt Lou paralyzed and struck dumb, and you all got no money to speak of and not much to eat. And there's that rickety windmill ready to fall on the house first storm comes along and squash you like

A Well of Living Water

bugs. Besides the water's gone bad in the well. And there you all are grinning like a pack of idiots!"

"Might as well laugh as cry," said Margaret.

"Well, I'll find you a pure spring and I'll dig you a new well," Buddy said, "and I'll tear the windmill down before it drops on you. I'll plant you a garden and milk yore cow, but don't ask me to join in yore smiling. I know better."

"You don't join in nothing at all, far as I can see," Margaret mused. "You're too busy swallering your little pink and yeller pills and listening to your insides churn to even know who's in the world with you."

"How I live is my business."

"That," said Margaret, "ain't living."

Buddy gritted his teeth. He threw the ball over Garth's head and banged it off the washtub, giving it such a jolt the water sloshed onto Margaret.

Margaret tossed the ball to Garth, and when he caught it he laughed out loud.

"This ain't my ball," he said. "It's a orange!"

"Eat it, then," said Margaret, "whilst I sew up the cover."

She hung up the last of the clothes and fetching a needle, thread and a thimble from the house, sat down cross-legged like a tailor under the windmill.

Buddy stepped over to the fence, startling the half-grown shoats so that they ran off squealing in all directions. He climbed up and sat on the top rail, yawning.

"But this here is yore orange," Garth said. "It's yores from lunch. They was only one apiece and I et mine."

"That's all right. Eat it up."

Garth sat beside Buddy on the fence, peeling the orange with his thumb. He was a thin, delicate little boy with big eyes like Enid, their mama. His hair was dark and curled at the temples like hers, and his smile was Enid's except now his front teeth were gone.

"I'm going to be a Big League's pitcher," Garth said. "When I'm a Big League's pitcher, then the kids won't say to me, 'Yore grampa's ghost is down in Trent pumping gas.'"

"You can't learn to throw a curve with a lopsided ball."

"I'll be a pitcher, though. Margaret says so. She says I'm special."

"What makes you so special, does she think?"

"My orange trees."

Buddy hadn't been paying attention. He opened his eyes wider and looked at Garth.

"Which orange trees is that?"

"The ones in my ears."

Buddy took his cap off and scratched his head.

"I don't see no orange trees," he said cautiously.

Garth giggled. "They're inside. You got to get close and look down in. Margaret seen one there after I et my first orange. And others has come since. She says they're a sign."

"Well, that's the biggest bunch of bullshit I ever heard!" Buddy declared.

He almost fell off the fence turning around fast to yell at Margaret. "Yo're filling Garth full of crap," he called over to her where she sat with the shadows of the windmill's legs striping her face.

"I got sassafras growing in my ears," she told him, "from drinking tea and chewing leaves."

"What's Buddy got in his?" Garth asked her when she came up to them with the mended ball.

Margaret climbed two slats of the fence and peered into Buddy's ear.

"Pigweed," she said. "Buddy's got pigweed growing in his ears from sitting in the piglot."

Buddy jumped down off the fence and grabbed Margaret's plait. "You're the sassiest girl I ever met," he said.

"That's a compliment I paid you," she cried, pulling away. "Pigweed's amaranth and that's everblooming. It's a sign. Folks that's got it ain't ever going to die. It's in there, honest. You just never knowed it."

"You're just chock full of sassy remarks, ain't you?" said Buddy.

And he wrestled Margaret to the ground and Garth, beside himself, jumped on top of them both.

"Margaret is so dumb," Buddy panted to Garth, "she don't know where people leaves off and plants and animals starts in. She thinks she's part toad and part owl and part sassafras root."

With a stiff yank, Margaret pulled Buddy's cap down over his face, and while he clawed at it, she slipped her hair out of his fingers and away she went across the yard with Buddy, mad as blazes, hot after her.

Around the house Margaret ran and down to the cowshed where she balanced around the edge of the watering trough, and then back up to the piglot with Garth shouting all the while and Gibbet shooting around and around the yard with her tail fuzzed up big as a coon's.

Bud judged he had her when she came up against the fence, but she sidled along it and over to the windmill and commenced to climb the iron ladder up the side. Buddy went up a rung and grabbed for her ankle. Then up another rung and almost got a grip on her heel, but she was too fast for him. On up she went and

A Well of Living Water

he after her, panting for breath.

She climbed to the top and crouched there just under the turning blades, laughing down at him. Halfway up, Buddy looked away from Margaret, down onto the roof of his Aunt Lou Fowler's house and beyond that, down the hillside into the valley.

He saw the setting sun raised up into the sky again as if by magic. There it blazed, dazzling his eyes so that he turned dizzy and had to hang on tight and lay his forehead against the cold iron of the ladder to keep from falling.

In the dark that rolled over him, he felt Margaret's hands on his shoulders guiding him down, shaking him awake.

2.

When Buddy came in from digging at the new well of an evening, Margaret put supper on the table and after they had eaten, Buddy took paper and pencil and drew a picture to show how he was sinking the shaft and how many inches the drill had gone down that day, and he put a line where he thought the water lay, and they each guessed how many more hours of drilling it would take to strike it.

While they talked, the dark came out from the walls and up from the floor like a flood rising, until the only light was the flicker from the cookstove door dancing red across the linoleum.

Then Margaret lit the coal oil lamp and set it in the middle of the kitchen table, and Buddy looked at each of their faces picked out by it, Margaret's and Garth's and his Aunt Lou Fowler's. It seemed to him that the light in his aunt's face came not from the lamp but from inside itself, and he remembered how she had rocked him when he was little.

At bedtime, when Garth walked around the table and kissed her goodnight, Aunt Lou reached out with her good arm and hugged him. Next Garth kissed Margaret and then Buddy. His lips on Buddy's cheek felt like butterfly wings.

"I'm down twenty-one feet and about to hit water," Buddy said early one evening just after supper, "but a goddamn bolt got lost off the drilling head and tomorrow's Sunday. We'll have to pay an extra day's rent on the well driller."

"The stores in Trent are open Saturday night if you got the energy to tramp down the hill," Margaret said.

Buddy scowled. "I got more energy in my earlobes than you got in yore whole body," he told her.

A Well of Living Water

"Help me tie up the tomatoes and I'll go along with you," Margaret said. "So I can carry you home if you give out."

They went into the garden they had made behind the house, and Margaret tore strips from an old sheet and he held up the vines while she tied them to the stakes. She was quick and deft and always ready to tie before he got the vine lifted.

When the last vine was tied, Margaret took the remains of the sheet and before he caught her purpose, knotted it around his ankles and away she ran down the hill past the new well shaft.

By the time he kicked loose, she was a quarter of the way down Fowler's Mountain. He tore off after her, going all out. The wind whistled past his ears. The bushes and trees went by in a blur. The blood pounded through him, setting his skin glowing. He began to whoop and holler. His voice soared out over the valley and echoed back.

He caught up with Margaret at the bottom of the hill just before the last dip and passed her, still shouting. She grabbed hold of his shirttail and pulled him off stride and herself with him so that their legs flailed and they stumbled down the last slope, fell and rolled together, gasping, in the long grass.

Their hands and arms were fragrant from the tomato vines. The sweat from their flushed faces ran together as he leant over her and when he kissed her, her mouth tasted of salt.

They scarcely recognized Trent. The village was transfigured. Strings of light bulbs covered with paper lanterns hung over every street, and every street was full of people.

"Look at them blue and red and orange and yeller faces!" Margaret whispered. "I can't name a soul amongst them, they look so strange, like they came up from hell or down from heaven, one!"

A great breathing sound of talking and laughing beat on their ears. Buddy could scarcely push through the crowd. He took hold of Margaret's hand to keep from losing her.

He couldn't find the hardware store. He dragged Margaret up and down while he stared open-mouthed at all the buildings.

"That's it there, Buddy," Margaret said. "Right in front of you. It's purple instead of white is why you don't see it."

Inside, all was ordinary. He bought a nut and bolt and stuffed them, wrapped in brown paper, into his pocket.

When he and Margaret stepped out the back door, there was the street fair again. A great circle of people was turning around the parking lot. A fiddler played while all the people lifted their feet in time to the music.

"This's what they used to call the 'Old Country Dance,'" Margaret shouted. "My ma and pa danced it when I was little."

Buddy wanted to duck back into the hardware store, but before he could turn around, both he and Margaret were swept into the circle and must stamp their feet and sing like the rest.

So then it was around and around, panting and laughing. Streaks of light and threads of sound. And hands touching hands. First the people clapped and then they hit their heels against the ground and a one two three four, around they whirled and took hold of hands and so around and around. When the fiddle sang the fastest an allemande began, right hand left hand and on around the circle. First Buddy took Margaret's hand and she passed by him and he took another hand and another.

At last, his head spinning, he went with closed eyes grasping over and over again a hand that was always the same, always different.

Even when Buddy broke loose from the dancers, he wasn't rid of the street fair, because nothing would do Margaret but he must throw baseballs in the stalls and knock the milk bottles down for her.

He threw and threw until his arm felt strong and warm and alive, and then he rattled down all the bottles and Margaret clapped her hands and cheered.

"Pick your prize!" the man said, but Buddy had another ball to throw and he begged to keep that instead, wedging it into his pocket where it pressed against his thigh as he walked.

When they got out of town away from the colored lights, Buddy knew they had delayed too long. Night was on them. He let go Margaret's hand and his face and his palms commenced to sweat.

"You and yore goddamn milk bottles," he said, with his teeth gritted. "Now we got to walk home in the dark."

"What you fretting for, Buddy?" Margaret said. "Ain't nothing going to hurt a body with amaranth in his ears. Anyhow, the moon'll be up in a half hour."

"Traveling this interstate on foot," said Buddy, "is like tramping through a fucking open grave."

But she was right. As they went on, the sky above the hills grew lighter and lighter until all at once the moon rose full and bright and turned all the trees silver and the road into a river of light.

Beside him Margaret jumped and twisted, lifting her feet and flinging out her arms. Buddy thought she'd gone crazy until he saw she was watching her moon shadow behind her, making it cavort on the road.

He saw his own shadow moving. Then Margaret's merged with his so there

A Well of Living Water

was only one shadow for the two of them. He was uneasy until they moved apart and he saw his own shadow clear and to itself again.

3.

The next morning Buddy got up whistling before daylight. He walked down the hill to the watering trough by the cowshed for a morning wash, but someone was there before him.

Margaret stood by the edge of the trough, her clothes in a pile at her feet, sponging herself with the water where it bubbled clear and fresh from the pipe.

The rising sun shone red on her wet skin and he saw the golden hairs on her arms standing up with the cold. Gibbet was crouched on the edge of the trough, her neck stretched out, drinking daintily.

Buddy came up to Margaret swiftly and she saw him too late to cover herself, but instead looked back at him motionless with her head raised like a deer.

For a while they stood quietly. Then he reached out and touched her belly, small and round like a new melon, and the hair beneath jeweled with drops of water.

She moved away from him gently.

"Well, you caught me out and that's my own fault," she said. "But looking is all you'll do, Buddy."

Then she threw back her head and laughed.

"I came out here so's not to wake up your Aunt Lou with that squeaky kitchen pump," she said. "I didn't plan on giving a show."

For here came the sheep down the hill for their morning drink, and the cow and her calf out of the shed, all watching Margaret as they came.

"You got a fine body, Margaret," Buddy said, and his voice was gone hoarse.

"I was the runtiest kid at the orphanage," Margaret said, "but all of a sudden I grew bigger than any of them. Folks as knew her says I favor my ma now. She was a tall big-boned woman."

Buddy felt that the dawning sun behind him was suddenly putting out the heat of noontime. It beat on his pole, on his shoulders and on the nape of his neck. It flowed down his back into his thighs like boiling water, and there was nothing he could do to stop it.

He saw Margaret narrow her eyes, watching him.

"Was you ever baptized, Buddy?" she asked him all at once.

He nodded, scarcely understanding her, and took a step closer to her.

"Well, that don't count because you wasn't never baptized like I'm going to baptize you," Margaret said, and before he could back off she grabbed him by the hair and pushed his head down into the watering trough.

"I baptize you," she said, "in the name of all these here sheep and cows and in the name of this ironweed and them pink and red hollyhocks and in the name of Trent and Kimball County. You was dead but now you live, you was lost but now you're saved. Hallelujah. Amen."

At every other word or two she dunked him, so that by the time she had finished he was groggy and spluttering and mad as hell.

Before he got the water out of his eyes and ears and mouth, she had grabbed up her clothes and was gone.

When Buddy got himself dried off he was over being mad. Instead, he felt ready to tear into the drilling with all his might. As he got out the new bolt and fixed the drill head, he thought, 'This is the day I'll bring in the well.'

He sat back on his heels and shook his fist at the windmill.

"Down you come," he said. "We're done with you, you spidery old bastard!"

4.

Buddy drilled two hours before breakfast. When he stopped, he was down twenty-seven feet. He remembered to get the baseball from the barn and take it up to the house for Garth.

They had a good meal. Margaret had baked bread, and she cut the warm loaf and gave each of them a slice, and she gave Buddy the heel. When Buddy poured out the milk, foaming and fresh, into the glasses, the wind blew in at the door and lifted his hair as if a hand had touched him there.

Once Garth had the baseball, he couldn't sit still. He left the food on his plate to run outside and toss the ball into the air. He was back almost at once, pulling on Buddy's shirttail.

"Come play catch," he said.

And nothing would do him but Buddy must come until Margaret said, "Leave Buddy eat. He's hungry and tired from drilling. I'll play with you a spell."

As Buddy ate, he listened to Garth and Margaret calling to one another in the yard. When he had finished, he stepped outside and fed Gibbet the scraps.

A strong breeze was turning the windmill, making it grind with a great deal of noise. Buddy's pants flapped against his legs. He saw grey clouds piling up over Fowler's Mountain and felt a drop of rain.

A Well of Living Water

The sudden hushing of voices puzzled him. Margaret and Garth and the ball were gone. The quiet pigs lay huddled together and the sheep stood like stones, sniffing at the wind.

Buddy started across the yard, his shirt fluttering. He had gone only a little way when he saw Margaret coming up the hill. As soon as she stood in front of him, she reached out and gripped both his hands.

"Garth just fell down the well shaft," she said. "He fell down all the way to the bottom. One minute he was there on the hill and the next he was gone."

Buddy could feel Margaret's body trembling. Her great shuddering came to him through her hands. It traveled into his hands and up his wrists and arms until he shuddered with her shuddering through his whole body.

It was Margaret who went down to Trent and gathered up the people while Buddy knelt in the nagging wind and called Garth's name down the well shaft. As he called, he wrung his hands.

Margaret came back riding in the fire engine beside the fire chief, Fred Kimes. The siren was going full blast. Doctor Joe Bryant was close behind, and all of the volunteer fire department. After them, people in cars and people on foot, men and women and children came straggling up Fowler's Mountain until nearly the whole village of Trent was standing around the new well, craning their necks and giving advice.

Buddy had sunk the well on a plateau fifty or sixty yards down from the house where the land and rock formation looked promising. Margaret had witched it with a peeled willow crotch and, though he put no stock in witching, the spot she picked matched with his. On this plateau, under heavy clouds, with a little rain dropping now and again, Buddy watched the crowd close and the volunteer firemen shake out their ropes and grab their picks and shovels.

When the firemen commenced scooping out a hole beside the well, Buddy had to move back from the shaft. As he squatted on the edge of the hole, a numbness spread from his stomach up into his chest and arms and down into his legs so that he felt stiff in every part, felt immobile and helpless as his Aunt Lou Fowler.

"Hope to God it don't rain," he heard the men say to one another.

As if it had heard, the sun came out, then clouded over again. Sun and cloud. Cloud and sun. But the wind never let up and the windmill never stopped creaking.

"More men're coming," Doctor Joe told him.

There the old man stood with his shock of white hair and his big stomach, looking and sounding to Buddy exactly as he had the day he delivered Garth into the world.

Buddy made a noise in his throat. It was as if he'd forgotten how to talk, he had been crouching there so long in silence. Then he said,

"I dug Garth's grave. There it is. I dug it myself."

Then men came pushing in between Buddy and Doctor Joe, demanding, "How're we going about this, Doc?"

Their shoes and clothes were caked with dirt. They sank their picks and shovels into the ground at their feet and scratched their heads and swore.

"How deep is that well shaft?" Chief Kimes boomed out as he joined them.

"Twenty-seven feet. Didn't Buddy say twenty-seven feet?"

"Yes."

"Then we've got to dig."

"Dig. Yes."

"Let's get some sense into this operation," Chief Kimes shouted.

"Hell, yes. Every time I sink a spade somebody cracks me in the gut with an elbow."

"Let the chief talk though. Quit yer bellyaching."

"Somebody's got to organize this business and be pretty damn quick about it, I say."

"First," said Chief Kimes, "you three men help Doc work that oxygen hose down the well shaft and we'll give the kid some air. Then we'll dig in shifts of five until we get this crater down within a few feet of the bottom of the well shaft. Then we'll sink a lateral tunnel to where the boy is."

"Let's get the bucket crane from down in Trent at the Olan Plant."

"No. We'd have a cave-in."

"It'd go a whole hell of a lot faster."

"Let them go get it," Chief Kimes said. "We can use it a while. Not for long, but at the top here."

"All I hope is that boy don't panic and try to claw his way out," Doctor Joe said, sighing. "The soft dirt'd bury him in two seconds."

"Don't the damned wind keep on and keep on!" Buddy heard the men say. "It's sure to rain. Look at them clouds."

"Let's get down there," they said. "Oh God, let's get on down."

The bucket crane roared up Fowler's Mountain. After it deepened the crater, the men jumped in and dug with shovels until they were spent and shaking and coated with mud. Then other men took their places. The clouds overhead gathered and rolled up the sky. The wind cut and whined.

Buddy could see that the men worked with a terrible concentration, shoulder to shoulder, silent now for the most part, saving their breath, striving together, glancing at the sky from time to time, and at the well opening. Just before dark,

A Well of Living Water

Margaret and the other women brought sandwiches down to the men and thermoses of hot coffee. A dozen coal oil lanterns were lit, and as many carbide lights, and through the night the men kept digging.

Time and again as the night wore on, Buddy started up out of his strange frozenness like a man come awake from a dream, jumped into the pit and dug with a pick or a shovel or with his hands, clawing at the dirt with his fingernails until sweat soaked his shirt and dirt matted his hair and crunched between his teeth. He dug furiously until the men came and pulled him away, shaking him gently, saying,

"Lay off, Buddy. For godsake, lay off. That ain't the way to go at it. You'll cave in the works, sure."

After several hours of work, Chief Kimes called a halt.

"The dirt's shifting down there," he shouted. He stood beside the shaft in his undershirt, covered with mud, his hair sweat-glued to his forehead.

"How's the tube, Doc?"

"It's still open," Doctor Joe said tiredly. "Oxygen's still going down."

"Let's put down the hook," Chief Kimes said.

"What if it starts a dirt slide?"

"We got the oxygen tube down all right. If the boy could hang onto the hook, we could pull him up out. Or if we could catch it in his clothes."

Buddy watched the men lower the hook and pay out the rope. It went down twenty-some feet, then caught and stopped. The men pulled up, lowered again, pulled up. The rope rubbed, worried like a line nibbled by a fish. It tightened. A cry went up from the crowd. Then the pressure on the rope was gone. They lowered it again and again with no result.

"We'd best pull it up," Chief Kimes murmured at last.

"He took hold of it that once, though," the men said. "Did you feel it?"

"Maybe," said Doctor Joe. "Maybe it caught on his clothes. Anyway, he couldn't never hang on strong enough for us to pull him out, and seems it won't catch again."

Buddy stood on the crater's edge, his knees shaking now, his palms marked with blisters. It was past midnight. The wind had fallen at last, but the sky was still overcast.

"This here's taking too long," he heard the men say. "We should of dug quicker. Like as not we're already too late.

"He can't still be alive, you know."

"It's seventeen hours he's been down there."

"They ain't been no sign nor sound for a god-awful long time."

Chief Kimes drowned them out, bawling, "We're down far enough. We can start to bore the tunnel."

Buddy watched a handful of picked firemen begin the delicate business of putting down the lateral tunnel.

The digging went on, growing slower and more careful. Now just three men were working, lying full length in the earth, making a human chain, until only the last man's boots showed.

The three firemen who had been digging came out of the tunnel and stood with their heads together talking to Chief Kimes. Silence settled over the people watching. It was as if they all held their breath. Buddy climbed down into the crater.

"How long is it?"

"Fifteen feet."

"You've about reached him then."

"Yes," Kimes told Buddy, "but the goddamn dirt's just shifted again. Their shoulders are sticking against the sides, but they're afraid to widen it for fear of a cave-in."

Buddy leaned over and peered into the tunnel.

"That's wide enough for me," he said, measuring it with his eyes. "There ain't none of yore men small as I am. I could get down."

Chief Kimes took off his cap and blotted his forehead with his arm, the while staring at Buddy. All the men looked at him and no one said anything. Finally Doctor Joe cleared his throat.

"One mis-move and you'll kill Garth and yourself in the bargain," he said.

Buddy's palms turned clammy and his breath came short and quick, but he said, "I'll go down."

"You'll have to go slow all the way and take care when you break through," Chief Kimes said, "or it'll bury you both for certain." Then he added in a lowered voice, "It's a good bet you'll not come out alive, no matter what you do. Just so you understand."

They tied a rope to Buddy's ankles and gave him a cap with a light fastened to it, and he lay flat on his belly in the dirt at the bottom of the crater and crawled into the tunnel. It was a tight fit. He wriggled his body forward, twisting along as a snake moves, pulling himself ahead with his hands.

The numbness was gone out of him. He had good command of his body, except that now and again spasms shook him because he was afraid. One inch, two, a foot, three feet. The sweat dripped off his chin onto his fingers. He went forward slowly, slowly, listening for the crack and sigh of a cave-in.

Before long the moist walls hugged him so tight he had to use all his strength

A Well of Living Water

to pull himself forward. At certain spots, he was forced to widen the tunnel. His hands began to bleed from the digging.

Once Buddy thought he heard a sound of dirt slipping and he froze, but it was only his own breath rasping in his throat. He went on crawling down bit by bit, slanting toward the bottom of the well hole along walls that shone like living hair and bore the marks of fingers, where the men who had dug the passage and who were standing above now watching and waiting had clawed the mud.

The fingermarks were the last sight he saw before a clod of dirt fell on his cap and knocked out his light.

A minute, two minutes Buddy lay still in the blackness, squeezed by the walls of the tunnel. Slowly his limbs began to stiffen. His tongue clove to the roof of his mouth. All his skin turned chill with an icy wetness. About him the dark grew heavy, smothering. Impossible to go on through that dark. Impossible to go back. He lay with his face in the dirt and a sob broke in his throat.

Almost at once, he thought he heard an answering sound. He lifted his head, leaned forward. Nothing. He'd imagined it, then. His breath was loud in his ears, hoarse and ragged. He thought the sound came again.

Dragging himself on with his elbows, he moved toward Garth, toward the place hidden in dirt and darkness where Garth lay wedged at the bottom of the well shaft.

A quarter of an inch, half an inch. His thoughts focused so intently on Garth that his muscles commenced to cramp and ache as Garth's muscles were surely cramping and aching. His breath came hard as Garth's was coming hard.

He thrust toward Garth with all his strength until he lost the feel of the tunnel around him, lost even the sense of the dark. There was only Garth up ahead and he, Buddy, flowing toward Garth and Garth reaching toward him like light flickering, like water running until of a sudden he felt himself fill with the boy and felt Garth fill with him so that there was no longer any separation.

Buddy continued his great straining toward Garth in the well shaft until he felt a tugging at his ankles and knew they were beginning to pull him back. At that he cried out and lunged forward, so that the fingers of his right hand reaching before him struck into a wall of dirt and crumbled it. Beyond he touched warm flesh. Buddy grabbed hard with another great forward lunge and a slap of both hands. Instantly a sharp pull at his ankles jerked him back up the tunnel into the open air.

Buddy knelt, stunned, at the bottom of the crater. Below him the opening of the lateral tunnel was gone, knocked in by the feet of the men who had pulled him out. The dirt kept rattling heavily down where the opening had been. Both Buddy's hands were still closed in a grip on Garth. The boy's eyes were open. He looked

A Well of Living Water

at Buddy and began to cry.

Trembling, Buddy raised himself, lifting the boy in his arms. Garth's body was rigid as if he were a boy of iron. His jaw was clenched, his eyes bloodshot and remote. But there was no dirt in his nose or in his mouth. And he was alive.

They came to him then, the other men, jumping into the crater from all its sides. They came shouting, their faces smeared with mud, their hair matted with sweat, their eyes bleary patches of white. They laid hold of him with their blistered hands and brought him and Garth together up out of the crater.

Buddy looked about him, blinking. Behind the men, peering over their shoulders, stood more men and women and children, and every soul was smiling so that the hillside was filled with smiling people and he, himself, standing in their midst, was smiling.

Climbing the hill carrying Garth, Buddy was weak and shaking, covered with cuts and bruises, tired out and hungry. Margaret came down to meet them, shading her eyes against the rising sun. When she took Garth, Buddy saw the boy whisper in her ear.

The three of them went on up to the house together, Margaret toting Garth astraddle of her right hip.

"He says," said Margaret, "that you've got pigweed in yore ears, Buddy, whether you know it or not. He seen it whilst you was carrying him up the hill."

ANNABEL THOMAS is a former elementary school teacher and journalist now living and writing in Ashley, Ohio. Her stories have won the O. Henry Award, and her collection, *The Phototropic Woman* (University of Iowa Press, 1981), won the University of Iowa Award and the PEN Center Award for short fiction. Her stories have appeared widely in such journals as *Prairie Schooner*, *The Ohio Review* and *The Literary Review*.

Her writing has been praised by Victoria Aarons for its human insight: "Through her characters Thomas explores self-knowledge, knowledge of the world, and the ability to know—to understand—others," and for its vision: "Thomas' characters find salvation in those things beyond thought, those elements that derive their strength from a physical, tangible reality, a reality that exists on an entirely different level than everyday concerns" (*The Literary Review*).

Jonathan Yardley recognizes her "affinity for the grotesque; many of her characters are slightly off center, out of touch, off in their own worlds. Yet, like other writers who frequently employ the grotesque—Flannery O'Connor, Doris Betts, Harry Crews—she finds universal themes in their odd, seemingly twisted lives" (Philadelphia Inquirer). Closer to home, Annabel Thomas' work exhibits a kinship with her fellow Ohioan Sherwood Anderson in its whimsical and tender treatment of rural life and its ultimate recognition of our shared humanity.

Moonless Place

Jack Matthews

> It's death to hate a poet,
> It's death to love a poet,
> It's death to be a poet.
> *Ancient Irish triad*

© copyright 1993
Jack Matthews
Moonless Place

PROF. HUGH DEVLIN'S STANDARD LECTURE ON THE WORD "GOTHIC"

By now we have read five Gothic novels, and have discussed them, and have therefore learned something about the *genre*. We have also discussed those features of Gothic that evoke such a deep and widespread response among so many people. Our most popular holiday is Halloween, which is essentially Gothic. It appeals to all ages because it is focused upon concealment and pretense, thus schooling us in the never-ending lessons of appearance and reality, persona and self...but also because it exploits certain Gothic values.

Nothing that has had such a prolonged effect as the Gothic tradition should be ignored; and it is time we pause in order to consider the term "Gothic" very closely and try to define it for our purposes. This will be the burden of my lecture today, and I will remind you that I have given considerable emphasis to the principle that as educated people we should always attend very closely to the labels we use, for when we don't, all discourse begins in confusion. Part of attending to them requires us to understand their past meanings, for our words were not invented this week or this year, and they did not come out of nothing—they came out of the past, and most have long, rich heritages that are necessary for an understanding of their plenary meaning.

Therefore, in today's lecture, I will try to clarify what we mean by the term

Moonless Place

"Gothic." The word originally referred to certain barbaric Germanic tribes that once spread over most of Europe. Some of you will have read that the Goths overran Rome in the early centuries of the Christian era. Their influence was so great, that other barbaric tribes spoke their language. Among these were the Vandals, eponyms of that irrationally destructive behavior which is so familiar a part of our world that we still have need of a word to denote it.

Perhaps you are aware that there was once even a Gothic alphabet, modeled somewhat on the Greek. In the fourth century, a bishop named Wulfila, who lived in the region of the lower Danube, translated the Bible into Gothic. And printers and typophiles still refer to an old-fashioned, heavily ornamental black letter typeface as "Gothic." But while the word can be traced back to the European tribes in the dark dawn of those early centuries, our use of it today has little to do with them. It derives rather from a style of architecture that flourished almost a millennium after Wulfila's Gothic translation of the Bible.

You have all heard of Gothic architecture, probably in the form of Gothic cathedrals. There are many vestiges of this style even today, most of which are "Neo-Gothic" Victorian churches or houses—and a few of the older buildings on our campus—built during the Gothic revival of the 19th century, and recognizable by their pointed arches, rib vaulting, flying buttresses, towers and spires. You all recognize Gothic "cathedral windows," which were deliberately designed to be high and narrow for good structural reasons, for the outer walls of cathedrals were supporting walls that required as much stability as possible in order to sustain those towering and massive edifices of stone that climbed so high, by medieval standards, into the heavens.

Gazing upon such a cathedral, one might be tempted to connect the words "spire" and "aspire," but the words are unrelated. And yet it has been said that the Gothic cathedral's intricate verticality symbolizes a yearning toward God and Heaven—which is plausible enough, for the symbolism refers to the inspiration behind their creation, and not to the architecture itself or to any specific theology. The Gothic sensibility was of great influence, and one can see its architectural forms reflected even in the Gothic black letter typeface I have referred to—most familiar to some of you, perhaps, in the old German type that prevailed in German texts before the rise of Hitler.

Here, in this architectural style, we can detect the Gothic spirit that is so important a part of the novels we have been reading. Now, let me ask you: how is it that what we think of as "Gothic" literature derives from an architectural style? How can a sort of building—specifically one that is characterized by pointedness and intricate verticality—relate to the ghostly tales that have so far preoccupied us this quarter? To put it simply and reductively, what is there that connects buildings and ghosts?

I do not see any hands raised, so I will tell you. A belief in ghosts requires a second room. Whatever room we are in at any time cannot be haunted, for we can see that it is not. We can see all that is there to see. The room is all presence, which is the habitat of signs rather than symbols. But like abstractions, the presence of a ghost is always, paradoxically, a sort of absence. Thus, if there is another room contiguous to this one we are in, and there is a door between these two rooms...the instant that door is closed, part of our imaginations is trapped in that other room.

And if there are many rooms, the possibilities for fearful and inscrutable presences are compounded. We can believe in ghosts providing they are thought of as being elsewhere. The instant they are fully present, the instant they are here, they cease being ghosts—or at least that sort of presence always to some extent absent, thereby troubling us by its ambiguous character. This explains why the door is a common symbol in literature, for it is a symbol of that which is hidden— which, I will remind you, is what the word "occult" means—and it is in hidden places that mystery resides and ghosts can be thought to exist.

But if this is so, why didn't Gothic literature thrive during the Gothic period itself? There were, of course, ghost stories at that time; but then, there have always been ghost stories. Most of these are surely forgotten, but some remain and are often classified as folklore—although there are a few examples of more authentically literary ghosts and goblins that have come down to us. Still, the Gothic novel, as we know it, was not born until several centuries past the decline of Gothic architecture.

The answer to this second question is connected with the answer to the first. To be effective or believed in, ghosts must be distant from us. Just as they can exist in another room in a way that they cannot exist in this room, so, correspondingly, they can exist in the past as they cannot exist in the present. Their removal in either space or time is a form of required distancing, necessary for "credibility" within a fictional context. One can of course read a good ghost story and "believe in it" while reading it without having the least temptation to believe literally in ghosts outside of the story.

Why should an old castle with mossy stone walls and deep-vaulted ceilings and echoing chambers be a felicitous and rightful habitation for ghosts in a way that a recently constructed Exxon station or McDonalds Drive-In Restaurant or Elementary School is not? The answer is: time and desuetude. When practical reasons for a building's structure no longer exist, it becomes something else in our imagination. No doubt at this very moment some inventive young author is writing a new "Gothic" novel about an old shopping mart that has been abandoned and weeds are already growing in the parking lots that were once filled with cars. Or perhaps his or her setting is an elementary school that was built only forty years ago, but is now abandoned, and the ghosts of the little children who once sat in their rooms singing out their ABC's can still be heard on nights when the moon is full.

Not only do most Gothic stories take place in buildings of more than one room, but these buildings are old...and they are likely to be abandoned. Desuetude is required, for the spirit of loneliness is necessary for us to feel the full effects of time and the mystery of the second room. Decay is also essential to this effect: old stone fountains covered with moss, wild shrubbery growing over benches that have not been warmed by human flesh for centuries, perhaps; great fissures in the building itself, which is as cold and dark as the tomb... all of these accoutrements are familiar, and we will find them abundantly evident in the stories of Poe that are assigned for next week.

Darkness is also necessary, of course. And it has been argued that the flourishing of the Gothic tale in the late 18th and 19th centuries is explainable partly because the electric light had not been invented. Probably this is so. But in some ways we have not advanced from those times as far as we suppose: turn out your lamp at night while you are studying and sit in the darkness of your room awhile, and you will discover that your ignorant and superstitious ancestors are nearer than you had thought. Light a candle and see how the light it gives trembles upon the familiar objects of your room, transforming them into things that do not appear quite the same. But as faintly illuminated as your room is by candlelight, it can never approach the darkness of the second room, for the instant you leave the second room—even if you leave it well-lighted—it reverts to an old vessel of uncanny possibility.

You will recognize all of the features I have been describing; they are fresh in your mind, for they have appeared in one form or other in all the novels we have been discussing during the term. You will also have noted that these features have been limited to scenic effects—stage setting and lighting, as it were. I have said nothing about the *dramatis personae*; I have not brought in pale maidens who are fey in the old sense of being doomed; nor have I brought in crazed old ghosts who walk the ramparts of the castle. There have been no moans at midnight or poltergeist shenanigans, and no stock narrator—usually a man or woman of limited imagination, upon whose sensibility the enormity of what is witnessed is scarcely altered as it passes into the reader's awareness.

Such conventional Gothic characters are important, and should be mentioned. But simply mentioning them is sufficient for our present purpose, for their

Moonless Place

function is often only perfunctory, and at worst, ludicrous. Gothic novels do not survive because of their characters, for even the living characters tend to be somewhat ghostly. Such novels survive for two quite different reasons—because of an idea and a permeant atmosphere that we find absorbing, mysteriously relevant and uncanny in its grip upon our imaginations.

What can explain this power? Even rational people (and I think of myself as rational, as most of us do) know this influence. As I have said, one can "believe in" a ghost story without believing in ghosts. But this is a curious truth, and should not be passed over too quickly; it deserves our attention. Partly, the reason for this has to do with our collaboration in the fulfillment of the meaning of the text. It has been argued that an unread text is not complete, not fulfilled—not really a text—until it is read. There is nothing intrinsically objectionable to this argument, although it is not the sort of argument that precludes its opposite. When we read a story, we play a game that has been first played by the writer. In short, we *pretend*; and we say that the degree of our pretense is an index of the story's "reality" for us. We collaborate by our "willing suspension of disbelief."

When we read a fictional narrative, we do so because we want to be deceived. We are asking for it; such a need is what inspires us to read stories. But how does this truth relate to non-fictional narratives—the account of an explorer in the Arctic, for example. Don't we go to that text wanting to believe, too? Of course; but in the latter, we are asked to believe in the account after we have finished it, whereas in a fictional narrative, the instant the book is closed, we are not only entitled to turn off our belief—to "pull the plug," as it were—we are expected to. And yet, a fictional narrative can affect us far more deeply and permanently than a non-fictional narrative. This is all very strange, and I invite you to think with me about it.

I have argued that Gothic effects require distance; the here and now does not provide an arena for them. Gothic effects do not fit what is present to the senses; they speak to us of that which is remote and thereby naturally difficult to understand. But this distance is not merely spatial; it is a temporal distance, as well; those other rooms which are the sole habitations for ghosts can be temporal rooms—those rooms of times we know as years and centuries. Thus, we believe in the ghost of Hamlet's father not only because of the magnificent scene in which he appears, but because the time of Hamlet himself is so remote from us that it is hardly distinguishable from the realm of ghosts. Who could be more ghostly than Shakespeare himself? Or Sir Walter Raleigh? Or Ben Jonson? In short, the more distant the Past—the less real it is, in quotidian terms—the more ghostly it appears.

Moonless Place

In this power to evoke remoteness, the Gothic performs a function that is essentially linguistic. Although Gothic literature is a *genre*, and we tend to think of it as occupying a rather exotic and irrelevant byway of culture, it accomplishes something in spectacular form that language accomplishes constantly, unobtrusively and essentially; for language is the essential symbolic instrument of remoteness. Whenever the language speaks itself through us or into our minds, it brings with it that which is not present to our senses.

No doubt some of you are stirring uneasily; I suspect that some of you are skeptical. "Does language always do this?" you ask. What if I take off my glasses, as I am doing now, and say to you, "I am taking off my glasses." What is distant about that, you ask. But I will turn your question around and say, "What is *linguistic* about it?" Your witnessing what I am doing makes the verbal report redundant. On the other hand, if we are talking over the phone and I say, "I am taking off my glasses"; or if I tell you, "I am thinking of taking off my glasses" or say, "I am taking off my glasses because my eyes are tired"? Various sorts of distance have been introduced, requiring the intermediation of language.

What does all this have to do with the Gothic spirit and our seemingly morbid, but certainly vital, interest in it? Let me remind you of our Arctic explorer, whose narrative of his adventures is intended to be truthful rather than fictional. For us to read with understanding what he has written, we must conjure up images and sequences and ideas from his words exactly as we would have to do if they were fictional. In the moment of reading, we must pretend that the past is happening again, so that we can witness it. But that "really happened," you will say, and the fictitious events did not. Nevertheless, that which has happened is gone forever, very much as that which never was.

I have not forgotten the word "Gothic" which has brought us together into this classroom. And I have not forgotten those special sorts of meaning we assign to it when we speak of it in a literary context. "Gothic" appeals to us because of its intense linguicity. (Is that a word? It is now.) In the extravagant claims that Gothic effects make upon our credulity, they perform radically what language does invisibly, inaudibly, and constantly. Ladies and Gentlemen, my claim in today's lecture is that one of the primary, and one of the greatest, appeals of Gothic Literature is to be found in its extraordinarily insistent linguistic function.

Why is this important? Well, if one concedes that language is the essential conceptualizing and civilizing tool, then the answer would seem obvious. But there is something deeper and darker at work in this: if we experience something overwhelming—perhaps some personal tragedy—we instinctively seek to fit whatever has happened into words. What is behind this instinct to express our most intense experiences? I believe it is our need to make our unique experiences fit into the language we have been given, for the language we speak is our primary instrument for understanding the world, to make sense out of the world, as if we could not sense things without it, as if we could not see, smell, taste, hear, and feel the things of this world without it. Furthermore, the words that can express what has happened to us have existed long before we have, and will exist after we have gone. They are, therefore, agents of order, continuity and reason.

This function has been called "time-binding"; but there is a deeper bond at work, for when we find the suitable words for what has happened to us, we have discovered our deep interconnectedness with others, living or dead. And if what has happened can find its expression in a literary form—a story or poem—our recognition is even more profound. Thus, literary forms are corrals for the nightmare—a truth which is manifest in the fact that most of the stories and poems we read are about events that have some capacity to wound, depress, or even terrify us, even when they are embodied in art ...but these events are far more terrible when they are not structured in narratives, remaining formless, vague, and horrifying in their uncertainty. Both reader and writer share in this ceremony, even though they seem to be on opposite sides of a linguistic act. Nevertheless, readers enlarge their sense of human consequences by reading what writers have imagined these consequences as being, for fiction is the art of seeing how one thing leads to another.

In this sense, then, art brings what it expresses into all the various rooms of meaning provided by its forms, all those rooms of meaning which others have fit with their private versions of confusion, meaninglessness and despair. The truths of our existence are such, that we have a chronic need to bring everything that is without form into the matrix of these known rooms, where we can see and touch them, and even express them in words.

Thus, to extend the metaphor that bonds this discourse together: our language games, along with those of literary forms, are the rooms we live in, and it is essential that we bring all the ghosts inevitably generated by our lives into these rooms in order to connect them with others, which is to say, clarify them and render them comprehensible. One name for this function is catharsis; but what we are here talking about is somewhat more than what is usually meant by that term.

I have argued that language, being essentially symbolic, is the instrument of remoteness; none of what it expresses is present, tangible, or immediate. Thus, it is through language that we reach out to grasp the world, but what we grasp is never sufficient, never quite enough. Always, we hunger for more. We are never sufficiently informed, even in the least matters.

Some of you might argue that when you are watching television your sense of the world is presented to you visually, without the intermediation of language. But this is only an apparent truth, for language has intermediated long before you switch on your TV set. Suppose what you see on the screen is a beautiful girl sitting on a veranda, the railing thick with flowering vines; and there is a pale blue mountain in the background. What could be more visual, less verbal?

And yet, your language has relentlessly, insistently taught you how to look at everything you see. The mountain would not be a mountain without the word and all its connections and associations for you; nor would the girl be a girl. And no matter how beautiful that girl is, no matter how we are moved by her beauty, we have learned it all, and mostly we have learned it through the prompting of language. Overwhelmed by that girl's loveliness, we are saddened and a little diminished when we contemplate that her beauty is conventional and socially programmed, therefore arbitrary and temporary.

This is a painful truth and goes against all sentiment. But if you question its validity, I suggest that you look at photos of bathing beauties from the 1920's or the portraits of Charles II's mistresses, or—for an even more radical departure from today's standards of beauty—photographs of women from cultures in which various sorts of bodily mutilation were once thought beautiful. Have we progressed far beyond this? Women with pierced ears please raise your hands if you believe that we have.

But this much is obvious, in a way; furthermore, my purpose here is not to provide arguments or documentation for the linguistic relativity theory. It is to show how the Gothic spirit connects with our essential lives, and to explore some of the possible reasons for the profound and almost universal fascination it holds for us. "Profound" is not too strong a word; nor is "universal"; remember, the word "Gothic" is the word that has brought us all together in this course, and we should think about the source of its magnetic attraction.

At the heart of Gothic stories is death. All of the accoutrements of ghostly horror are fictions projected upon that great and distant Silence that awaits us all. Even little children sense this, and take comfort in dressing up as and personifying ghosts and goblins, for when they step into their little costumes, they are not only transforming themselves from victim into victimizer, but participating in the creation of an image of the ultimate mystery, that which is both intimate to us and yet most remote from all we can understand. The thought of our eventually dying and becoming part of this remoteness is the source of terror—one which we strive to mitigate by domesticating it, just as we project familiar images upon those astronomically distant irrelevancies that loom over us and call them Ursa Major, or the Great Bear, or the Big Dipper—a star pattern that is fanciful at best, and limited to our own pathetically limited perspective. But to return to our Halloween children, who are younger, more vulnerable, more believing versions of ourselves: their embodying of remoteness, I will remind you, is the essential function of the symbol.

We are all fascinated by death. Nothing is more mysterious, more inevitable, more evocative of what is essential to our humanity. Although we usually dread the very thought of it, it is not in itself—or in its essential image—an evil. Beauty, love, goodness could not exist without death, although we like to think they could and behave as if they do. And yet, without the evanescence of the world and ourselves, what would there be to cause us to strive to live honorably or love one another?

We are mesmerized by the thought of death, and suspect that we are preoccupied with it even when we are least aware. We want to explore its boundaries; we want to stand at the edge and peer down into that abyss, as if by peering we might see something where all those who have lived before us have looked without ever once glimpsing anything that could be put into language convincingly and shared with others to their general satisfaction.

Our obsession with death extends to thoughts of suicide, which I believe is not only a normal, but a healthy notion for an intelligent being to entertain now and then. Please note that I am not recommending suicide as an *act*; rather, I am saying that its theoretical validity is something we should all acknowledge and be aware of. For, to speak practically, I can think of situations—a very, very few, but they are real—in which suicide would be preferable to life; and so can you. To ignore this is to ignore part of the wide spectrum of human options. Nowhere is Hamlet more himself, more human, than when he broods upon the *possibility* of self slaughter. Indeed, a few societies have sanctioned suicide: one immediately thinks of the ancient Romans, and old Cato, who we are told in MOBY DICK, "with a philosophical flourish, threw himself upon his sword" (I've often wondered what, exactly, that philosophical flourish *was*); and then there is the ancient Japanese tradition of *hari kari*. Most of us feel an instinctive horror in contemplating such acts; and this, too, is natural. But it does not eclipse that which those acts revolt from; nor does it obviate the theoretical validity of that ultimate act of defiance in a world turned wrong.

But if we can accept a theoretical justification for suicide, then are we not logically committed to an analogous theoretical justification of homicide? Some

Moonless Place

of you will deny that this is so; you will argue that we may have a privileged authority over our own individual lives, but not over others, and that while one of us may find our own life worth less than nothing (because of a terminal illness, let us say—choosing an obvious example), we have no legitimate perspective by which to judge another's life to be worthless.

And yet, there are many situations in which we find some people more "killable" than others. To choose another obvious example, if you are at war, those wearing the uniform of the enemy are surely more killable than those wearing your own uniform. Or if someone seriously threatens you or your loved ones with violence or death, surely you have a natural right to stop that person, even if it means killing him or her. Or if someone has violated someone who is close to you—let us say, a man has raped your wife or even a woman with whom you have a loving relationship—hasn't that person, that man, by that act alone proved himself killable in a way that you could not have known otherwise?

Our notions of "killability" are ambiguous, as they should be. In one sense, it is right that we believe that the lives of all people are equally sacred; it is right that we hold human life to be an absolute. But we know this is a fiction, albeit a very important one; for not all lives are equal. How could they be? How does the life of an elderly stroke victim in a coma compare with that of a healthy child with the prospect of years of useful life before him? It is good that we seldom have to face such a choice, but if we did have to choose which of these two should live at the expense of the other, would we not all agree? Or what about two people— "equally human" in the eyes of the law—but one with a psychopathic personality, and the other a well-adjusted, productive, kindly human being? Who would be judged more killable than the other?

This final turn in today's lecture represents the fact that it is not only language and death that are at the heart of Gothic literature, but language and murder. I plead with you earnestly to consider well what I have said, and what I have not said. I have not urged you to kill yourself or kill another. My lecture has been focused upon the word "Gothic," and through that, what may be termed the Gothic experience; and all that I have said must be judged in terms of its relevance to this course, along with the relation of our subject to the world we live in and pretend that we understand.

I have one last comment, however, about the word that brings us together. This word reveals how close we are to death and terror, how dangerously imminent murder is to even the most peaceful of creatures. Do you doubt it? Consult your dreams. Literature, like dream, corrals the nightmare, and thereby gives us a place for our most horrible possibilities.

Believe me, I speak to you as one who knows. Please heed my words, and do not commit yourselves casually to grotesque undertakings. We are all nearer to madness than we realize. "Mad enterprise lies just beneath our speech, an itch beneath the skin we cannot reach." Oh, what stories I could tell you! Which is to say, what notions, what possibilities! But now, you will understand, is neither the time nor the place.

And that will be all for today. Thank you.

THE DEAD GIRL'S MOTHER

When the woman phoned, she said, "You don't know me personally, but you did know my daughter."

Wary, Hugh Devlin said, "Oh, is that so?"

"Yes, I'm Elena Kolb's mother."

He inhaled; and then, exhaling, muttered, "I see." He cleared his throat and repeated, "I see."

"I'm sure you do."

Whatever she meant by that was unclear, but he groped for the right-sounding phrase, saying: "Of course I'm sorry about your daughter, Mrs. Kolb. She was...well, she was a student in my class. I guess you must know that or you wouldn't be calling me like this."

Calling me like this! God, he was blithering. "What I mean is," he went on, "obviously you know she was a student of mine or you wouldn't have called."

That was certainly no better, and merely by being repetitious seemed to weaken him almost physically; but what, exactly, was he supposed to say to a woman whose daughter less than a year ago had committed suicide in her dormitory on campus?

He continued: "You grope for some kind of understanding in something like this...I mean, when a fine young girl like...Elena does something so awful, so terrible..."

He let his voice dwindle, while the terrible woman at the other end of the line remained silent. *What in the hell does she want?* Two properties away, Greg Sherman whipped his lawnmower into a steady growl.

"In a way, that's what I wanted to discuss with you," Mrs. Kolb's voice went on. Emerging from heavy silences, she seemed already to have a way of sounding implacable. "I'd like to talk with you. Will you be in your office tomorrow?"

"Tomorrow? Well, If you'll hold on, I'll see if I can arrange it."

At that instant Hugh Devlin seemed to hear his voice echoing in the receiver, as if there had been no one else to hear. He had once been proud of his resonant tenor; but increasingly of late he distrusted some quality he could hear in it—as if his patience with different aspects of himself had a built-in longevity, a rate at which it would go wrong, showing that from the start it had been destined to betray him. Lately it was the inner echo of the voice itself—the messenger which brought him such dreary news—that had begun to irritate him.

He picked up the receiver, ending his brief hypocrisy just as the grandfather clock in the front room began to gong four times in its stately cadence over the sedate growl of Greg Sherman's lawnmower. He said, "Yes, I can meet with you tomorrow. I have office hours from nine to ten-thirty, but if that's not convenient, I can arrange another time, except for my afternoon class in..."

"No." Mrs. Kolb's voice slipped like a needle into the rich texture of his voice. "Ten will be fine."

He told her that was settled, then...without even resorting to the tactic of hedging and pointing out that he couldn't be sure whether he had a student appointment at that hour or not, because he sometimes wrote down appointments on his desk calendar on campus without remembering to put them in his breast-pocket notebook.

But the fact was, he knew very well he didn't have such an appointment and ten o'clock was free.

TIME DIMENSIONALIZES VALUE: OR, THE DEVLINS AT HOME

Having long ago exorcised his creative demons, Hugh Devlin lived a basically contented existence—surprisingly so, as measured by what he considered the modern world's mindless criteria for success and happiness. He was comfortable teaching his courses in literature and creative writing and watching the world of literary reputations flash and rumble on the screen of glitz and meretricious fashion. He had come to believe that even the most mature and best balanced writers are victimized by popular success, becoming instruments of their own cunning, and are soon left with little knowledge of the shared realities of others and how those realities fit into the human fabric. Though socially centrifugal, hence delusive, success inevitably devours itself...and yet, a true poem is a small light in the world's darkness. So it was only natural that Hugh Devlin came to believe that teaching English and creative writing courses at the college level was the most pleasant and useful way for him—not just to "earn a living," but to spend his life.

Along with his profession, his marriage and home life were uncommonly happy. While he and Lenora did not have children, they had each other and sensibly kept reminding themselves of this fact. They had remained warm and affectionate friends, as well as man and wife. They had met in college; and he recalled that the effect of his first glimpse of her was almost like being punched in the stomach. Although he avoided the vulgarity of personal reference, he liked to tell his students that there are occasions when such an old cliché as having "your breath taken away" comes near to expressing a literal truth.

As for Lenora, she liked to say that she had instantly fallen in love with what she'd once called his "big handsome Irish head"—a judgment that was privately and intimately hers, for his features were rather irregular and over-sized, so that people were more likely to think of him as pleasantly homely than handsome. Then, too, there was his wonderful voice. She had always been fascinated by it, along with his manner of speaking. This, too, was personal, because what struck others as pomposity had an elusive and antic eloquence for her. Which was typical, for Lenora's sharp and cunning wit found pleasure where others saw nothing but dreariness. Her responses were so unconventional that in certain wacky moods, even the crime rate and inflation index struck her as being somehow, essentially, hilarious.

She had always been this way. When they were students, she had been fascinated by Hugh's slow and careful solemnity—a manner so stilted and professorial it seemed utterly incompatible with the golden blarney of a wild Irish poet she thought his looks promised. And yet, hadn't those first crazy impressions been vindicated, after all, by their decades of happiness together? Hadn't the two of them managed to fashion a marriage that was so much better than most marriages today it was almost a different institution entirely?

Lenora was a clinical psychologist, now retired after twenty years of practice. She had retired early, worn down by her chronic exposure to human failure. She had begun to find so much misery demoralizing and could no longer renew herself as she once had. She was afraid that the accumulated despair, fecklessness and confusion of her patients might stain her mood permanently. She couldn't separate herself from their miserable litanies. Therefore, since Hugh's salary and eventual retirement—along with a few solid investments—would provide all the comfort they needed, she retired.

Just before retiring, she enjoyed telling their friends that she intended to spend long hours wallowing in the dreamiest, sappiest, most vulgar Gothic romances she could lay her hands on. She said it was her major sin and she intended to do it justice and give it all she had. "How could any serious-minded person ignore a *genre* that fascinates so many women?" she asked. And then, as if to cap it off,

Moonless Place

she added, "Not only that, poor Hugh can't stand the damned things, so how could I resist?"

This was true; but just because he wasn't tempted to read them, didn't mean he was unappreciative in other ways. His disapproval was practical, not theoretical, for he liked the *idea* behind Gothics. He said that a historic purview of any subject is interesting, because time dimensionalizes value. In pursuit of this idea, he became fascinated with the historical antecedents of modern Gothic romances and eventually designed his own course in Gothic Literature, which was constantly enriched and documented by Lenora's testimony regarding those living vestiges that clutter the shelves and bins of malls and supermarkets throughout the country.

Although Hugh Devlin had for years suffered from insomnia, both of them had enjoyed reasonably good health until Lenora developed a form of arthritis that settled in her left leg and stiffened it. Last Christmas, Hugh had given her a specially made malacca cane with three silver bands and a silver handle as big and solid as a door knob. "Now Limpy the Clown can limp in style," Lenora said; and Hugh told her that was a stylish attitude, which was the only way to do it, after all.

ELENA'S DIARY

At twenty minutes before ten, Devlin looked up from an essay titled "The Gothic Castle as Feminist Real Estate" in THE SALT CREEK QUARTERLY and was surprised by the woman's silent presence in the open doorway of his office.

"Professor Devlin?"

"Yes, and you're Mrs. Kolb. Please come in and sit down."

"I'm afraid I'm early," she said.

"No problem. Come in, come in."

She nodded and sat in the only other chair in his small office. She was young-looking, dressed elegantly in a tan skirt and blouse, with pale blue turquoise in her necklace and bracelet. Her hair was a mouse brown with gray in it, combed back behind her ears and held in place by two identical silver barrettes, also studded with turquoise. Her eyes were the same pale blue as the turquoise, creating an effect Lenora would have called "striking."

Unquestionably she was a handsome woman, in spite of age wrinkles and a slight puffiness around her eyes, which gave emphasis to the pale irises and seemed to belong to an interestingly older face. She sat gracefully and gazed at him without speaking, until Hugh shook his head and said, "Mrs. Kolb, I often tell my students that there are times when we're driven to clichés. As at the present moment. But I try to explain that clichés are not intrinsically, not *always* bad; they can damage otherwise good writing, true enough, and get in the way of clarity and vigor and all those commendable things...but the fact is, there are occasions when we're all driven to clichés as if they're...well, sorts of truth, that is to say, *formulas* of truth, which I guess they are, in a way. Because they're shared truths, which are, after all, probably the most important kinds. God, I hope you don't mind my babbling on and on like this, but the fact is..."

The fact was, he didn't know what the fact was, and simply sat there miserably aware that he was hot and uncomfortable and that the woman sitting opposite him didn't seem to be taking in a damned thing he was saying. And who could have blamed her?

He grabbed the bridge of his nose with his thumb and finger, and then dropped his hand limply into his lap. "Mrs. Kolb," he said in a slow, practical voice, "is there anything I can do?"

"I'm not sure," she said plopping each word down like a chess piece, "but that's why I'm here."

"*What* is why you're here?"

Mrs. Kolb frowned. "You see," she said finally, closing her eyes and touching the fingertips of one hand to her temple, "Elena...well, Elena kept a diary."

"Do you mean the journal she kept for my class?"

Looking troubled, she nodded. "Yes."

"I'm aware of the fact. It was an assignment for the course. I always assign a journal."

She nodded. "It was among her personal possessions they shipped back to me last year. I was surprised by some of the things I found in it."

"I see."

"Although her...her passionate ambition to be a writer or poet of some sort...well, that was certainly no surprise."

"I see."

She narrowed her eyes at him. "Really? *Do* you?"

"Well...I *think* I do. Of course, it's always hard to measure another's ambition." Hugh closed his eyes and ran his hand through his thick, curly hair. "Or passion."

When he opened his eyes, he saw that she was looking sharply at him. She said, "Professor Devlin, I've read it."

He nodded. "Well, of course you have."

Moonless Place

"There's so much I didn't know! I'm almost ashamed to admit it. My own daughter!"

He nodded. "Parents and children can be great mysteries to one another."

"Professor Devlin, Elena...well, I think you should know something I discovered while reading her diary—I'm convinced that she was writing about you."

An odd and ugly sort of thrill went through his stomach. "What are you talking about?"

Mrs. Kolb took a deep breath and looked almost defiantly at him. "In some ways, Elena was a very, very strange girl, Professor Devlin. I think you should know that."

Why should I know that? some translation of his own voice sang out deep inside his head. But he was confident that his expression remained dignified and perhaps just a little cold. As it had every right to be, God knows! Not to mention about *time*!

"Once years ago, when she was a very small girl, we were so close! I used to read to her every night. I read everything ; I suppose that's where it all began. But then, after her father left...well, the truth is, her father and I are divorced."

In this, as in almost everything he'd witnessed about this implacable woman, there was something indefinably odd; it was almost as if she were confessing to a bizarre and extraordinary secret, instead of stating a fact that was true of about half the adult population. As he often told his students: "Divorce has become an institution—not a happy one, but one whose existence can't be ignored. Therefore, as in all existential crises, we are fumbling around to define what it is that has descended upon us like a social plague. And it is this very lack of definition that intensifies the dismay and confusion and...well, *anguish* of all who are connected with it."

She sighed. "I'll never forget those long wonderful evenings when I would read to her! And how she'd snuggle up and want to hear more and more. She just couldn't get enough. She preferred it to television. Later, we drifted apart, of course. I suppose it's natural, in a way; still, it's all very sad."

Hugh said, "In my classes I always take great pains to distinguish between journals and diaries. Students often ignore the distinction." He waved dismissively, obliterating the intelligence of countless sophomores. "Or fail to grasp the distinction. But I emphasize that I want them to concentrate upon ideas and images, not the messy details of their personal lives."

Mrs. Kolb was shaking her head sadly. "Did you read her diary?"

"I'm sure I must have, Mrs. Kolb. Twice every term I ask to look at their journals. Let me see." He got out his roll book and with his index finger traced down the names of his 262 class to Kolb, Elena. "Yes," he said. "My records show that she kept her first conference with me."

"Yes," she murmured.

He paused a moment, and then it came to him. "Of course. That's why you wanted to see me. You want to pick up any other papers I might have of hers. Perfectly understandable, of course."

When she simply sat staring into his face without speaking, he rubbed his hand through his hair and babbled on: "Only, you could have just asked me for them, and I would have sent them to you. I mean, you didn't have to…"

He stood up and went to his file cabinet and began to shuffle through the motley clutter of tattered paper folders and plastic notebooks. He kept them stuffed horizontally in back of the metal dividers, unfiled and therefore not easily found. But he dug in vigorously, and while he was looking, he began to explain how he conducted his classes. "When they have their first conference, I look at their journal entries—but of course Elena wasn't…that is to say, she couldn't have met for the second one and…"

Appalled, he stopped and turned around to face the dead girl's mother. "*God, that's awkward!*" he muttered. "I'm really sorry, you know. I didn't mean to be so insensitive."

Finally she spoke, moving her silver-ringed hand to the side. "Oh, that's all right. That's not what bothers me."

What wasn't? He seldom felt so out of touch with a conversation he was engaged in. Had Elena herself been like this? He tried to remember, but he couldn't quite bring her image into focus. She'd killed herself just before the deadline for withdrawal from classes without a tuition penalty; so she could hardly have been in his class long enough for him to really get to know her personally.

He turned back to the file cabinet once again, and at that instant, came upon two of Elena Kolb's assignments and removed them. One was a character study and the other was simply the description of a room. Mickey Mouse assignments, to be sure; but as he liked to point out to his students, no writing assignment is really useless, because all assignments begin in the imagination and lead back to it.

He glanced at the papers briefly, then handed them over and returned to his seat. But Mrs. Kolb showed little interest in them. Putting them in her lap after a brief glance, she said, "Professor Devlin, I'm going to speak plainly. I have admitted that I had trouble understanding my daughter, but in reading her journal I came to an escapable conclusion: Elena idolized you. Did you realize that?

Idolized! And the most important thing in the world to her was...do you have any idea of what that was?"

The horror of what was coming seemed to scoop out the heavy reality of everything before him: his desk, the bookcases on the far wall, and the dead girl's handsome, silver-bejeweled mother sitting in the chair not over five or six feet away. He wanted to say, But I have so many students...!

"What?" he finally asked.

"She wanted to be a writer, Professor Devlin! She wanted to be a *poet!*"

Having expected something profoundly mysterious, he had a brief impulse to laugh at such bathos.

But Mrs. Kolb was intent upon a revelation she seemed to regard as being as ultimately inscrutable as marital divorce. She placed her open palm on her chest just below her throat and intoned: "Being a writer was more important to her than anything else in the whole, wide world! She wanted to be a poet all her life—at least for as long as I can remember. When I would read children's books to her, she listened so hard you could almost *hear* the intensity of her listening. She memorized poems, whole poems. She could recite them by the hour."

Then the dead girl's mother stopped, held her arms out and jangled her silvery wrists and fingers. "Oh, she was a strange girl!"

"We're all strange, Mrs. Kolb," he said.

But she was too intent upon her own banal revelations to find interest in his own banalities. "For as long as I can remember, she wanted to be a writer. A poet. Nothing else. Nothing else would do. To be a writer was everything to her."

Hugh clutched his chin with his hand and frowned. "Mrs. Kolb, there are so many students who want to be writers; but most are more interested in themselves as writers than in writing itself. Perhaps that is only natural, after all. But I can assure you that there aren't many who are willing to work hard enough and read enough and simply endure enough to succeed. Then, too, there is the great mystery of talent, which can't really be defined."

"I'm sure everything you say is true," Mrs. Kolb said, not sounding sure at all.

"None of us want to be forgotten," Hugh said.

She opened her eyes wide. "Forgotten?"

"We can't bear the thought that we're going to die."

"I'm not sure I understand. What does dying have to do with it?"

He smiled sadly. "Everything. You see, the intensity of being oneself...especially when you're young."

"Maybe you're right, only *I* can't remember being like that. Wanting to write poetry and stories would have seemed rather strange to me. In fact, if I can remember right, all I seemed to think about was sex." She paused a moment, blinking at what she said, and then laughed.

Hugh nodded. "Isn't it possible the two are connected?"

"*Connected*? Sex and poetry? Well, I suppose maybe they are, but I'm not sure *I* can see it."

"In a way, I'm thinking of sublimation, of course—only it's something much more elusive than that."

When she didn't respond, Hugh cleared his throat and said, "As a matter of fact, when I was Elena's age, I wanted to be a writer; and so did almost everyone I knew. Eventually, in graduate school, and later as a young instructor, I actually published quite a few poems. I even gathered them into a book, titled ROOMS OF SELF. But do you know what I tell people? I tell people that I published two dozen poems and a book that, so far as I could know, had been read by no more than twenty-five people...if one can assume that editors read what they publish."

Seeing the expression on her face, he shook his head. "But, good God, never mind that; I hope you'll excuse all this irrelevant gab. The point is that...well, not many young people have enough ambition and toughness and talent to succeed."

She fastened her look on him. "*Elena* did."

He frowned again. "Maybe you're right. Perhaps she did. But I assure you that the percentage is pathetically, bewilderingly, dishearteningly small...still, I'm willing to admit that perhaps she did."

"Yes," Mrs. Kolb said, nodding.

Hugh nodded, too. "Of course, even though I teach creative writing, I'm aware that I have no real authority to judge something so imponderable as talent." He said this with the clear implication that the dead girl's mother had even less authority to speak of such a mystery.

But she hadn't listened. "You did read her diary, though, didn't you? Or at least as much as was completed by the time you had your conference with her?"

He rubbed the back of his neck. "I'm sure I must have read her...her journal. And yet, with so many students, Mrs. Kolb, you really do have to understand..."

But this woman was obviously not interested in understanding. She said, "You must understand that Elena was a very, very strange girl. After her father left, she changed so much that I felt I hardly knew her. My own daughter!"

Saying this, her voice seemed to break a little, and Hugh gazed at her in fascinated horror, afraid she might cry out or start weeping or stand up and start throwing books on the floor.

But she got control of herself, and continued. "And then when I got her diary

Moonless Place

and read it, I learned things about my daughter that I find strangely troubling."

"Yes, you've said that," Hugh said. "But what things, exactly?"

She shrugged. "Oh, it'd be hard to put into words. Although there were some things that are perfectly clear."

"Yes?"

Frowning, Mrs. Kolb shook her head. "I've brought it with me, Professor Devlin, and I want to ask you to read it…the part you've already read, but more closely. And then the new entries. Right up to the end. "

"But why? Don't you realize…?"

"Oh, I know how busy you must be. But I think you really ought to read it because as I said, in a way it's addressed to you."

His head seemed to whirl as he listened to his own relentlessly articulate voice come to the defense. "Since I *assign* the journals, it's only natural to think of them as being addressed to me, in a way. It could hardly be otherwise. Students can't really keep a journal innocently, or even honestly, knowing that eventually I'm going to read it. As I often tell my classes, you can forget, but you can't unremember."

"I don't think I understand what you're saying."

"I'm trying to explain how everything we do establishes a context, but it happens within a matrix."

"I'm talking about what's written here." Not looking down, she tapped the notebook in her lap with a long polished fingernail.

Distractedly, he rubbed his hand through his hair. "I know. I know! I'm always doing that."

"Doing what?"

"Lecturing people. But when you've taught as long as I have, Mrs. Kolb, any question that has to do with…"

She was nodding into his sudden silence. Then she said, "Reading it, I was impressed by how much she loved the way you talked. She loved your voice. And she thought you knew so *much*; her mind was dazzled just by the fact of being in your class. For me, reading her diary was like getting to know two strangers, you and my daughter! While I was reading it, I realized that for Elena being a successful writer didn't necessarily mean becoming famous so much as it meant being able to be accepted by someone like you… to be able to satisfy the demands you made upon her as an artist."

An artist, he thought. And instantaneously, as if hearing his thought, Mrs. Kolb once again nodded.

MOONLIGHT COCKTAIL

Lenora was listening to some old Glenn Miller records. She loved to listen to them now and then, and when she was in the mood, as she liked to put it, she regretted that Hugh and she were one generation too late to have heard all of that velvety music from inside. It was an interesting thought, and Hugh would sometimes discuss it with her, drawing her out the way he would draw students out...doing so without calculation to manipulate, certainly; and certainly without anything like condescension. Only habitually, instinctively, in the way of one who has taught so long, loving the classroom so much.

Now, sitting in his study and half-aware of "Moonlight Cocktail" playing distantly in the house, Hugh sipped at a cup of English Teatime tea, opened Elena Kolb's journal and began to read. Vaguely he recognized her handwriting; it was small and fastidious, with the loops fat and generous, but as regular as if they had been drawn with a compass. Each entry occupied an entire page of the 6" by 9" green spiral notebook, as if the events of each day's deliberations could be boxed into one page with undeviating regularity. Although he considered interpretive graphology an utter imposture, it seemed hard to believe that such generous loops were those of a girl about to commit suicide.

Somewhere in the fourth or fifth entry, he paused and tried once again to remember exactly what Elena Kolb had looked like. He recalled a heavy, plodding, unattractive girl—short and blocky with jet-black hair cut in a Prince Valiant bob. Her hair was such a glossy black it could almost have been dyed. Her dark eyes were set too close together, giving her an intense, almost stupid expression that he thought would surely have discouraged any male from taking a personal interest in her. Although such things are, of course, imponderable. Because, hadn't Lenora at one time found him handsome? Still, it was ironic that such a plain and bulky girl should have a mother who was so much more attractive in her forties than she herself had been at nineteen or twenty.

Sighing, he went back to the journal, entering upon a long passage of embarrassing mediocrity—a self-indulgent, romantic outpouring of adolescent yearning and misery, the disgusting wail of discontent that everyone has to leave behind somehow, somewhere, on the long hard climb toward maturity. Like so many of his students, she began to impress him as being perhaps basically, or at least potentially, intelligent, but defiantly ignorant.

Reluctantly, and yet with something like a morbid fascination, he turned the pages. The taut neatness in the lines, utterly devoid of cross-outs and additions, had an effect of sterility. Students often filled their journals with sloppy expressions of uncontrolled energy—antic drawings and doodlings and garish splashes of color from felt tip pens and large letters spelling out obscenities or catchy phrases or the runaway names of lovers. But here there was nothing but a neat progression, a record of sensation following sensation, in which virtually every entry proclaimed the beauty of sunlight and flowers, the perfidy of mankind (but with a vocabulary far too unsophisticated for "perfidy"), the desolation of loneliness, and the majesty of night.

The majesty of night! Where had he gotten that? Certainly not from this poor dim girl's maudlin diary posing as a journal! And yet, knowing the issue of all those pages—where they were headed, perhaps even without her knowledge—Hugh Devlin sensed that this may have been the true subject of her discourse; it may have been the latent text of what she had been writing to him, alone, as if every entry had been part of a long and secret personal letter. For loneliness and poetry both come out of darkness and privacy, only the one comes forth more vividly than the other...and, some would say, travelling a vaster distance, emerging from a far deeper darkness into a far brighter light.

But the inescapable fact was, this time he could no more read her journal in a state of innocence than she could have written it thus. Indeed, he breathed to himself as he bowed his face over his cup of tea, it is true that you can forget but not unremember! And thinking this, it occurred to him that if he as her teacher had cast a shadow over every word written in her class journal, then, now, as he read it, the presence of both the dead girl and her mother could never be quite forgotten. That handsome woman with her jangling expensive turquoise jewelry must be aware that he was reading the journal that her daughter had kept almost to the very moment she had taken her own life...with sleeping tablets, as he suddenly remembered, and alone in her dormitory room on a Saturday night.

He found something very pathetic about her dying on a Saturday night, a night when her roommates and other girls of the dormitory were on dates or uptown drinking beer in one of the half dozen college taverns vibrating with rock music. But he was not surprised by the lack of reference to boyfriends in the diary, much less anything suggestive of a love life—because the girl he remembered was uncommonly homely and awkward looking. Nor did she refer to any boys, unless some male named "Ernest" was a boy rather than a man. But her reference to him suggested that he was a different, far older presence—a man who evidently lived in another town. Perhaps an uncle she'd known on a first-name basis, or maybe a remembered high school teacher. Her references to him seemed almost naked admissions of loneliness, because whoever he was, Ernest was not accessible. No wonder the poor girl had been driven to poetry, as had so many others before her...as had *real* poets, for reasons that were not entirely dissimilar.

By the time he finished reading, he felt something almost like exhaustion. He sat there for a while, looking through his study window upon the darkening lawn. To think of all that darkness and misery and passion existing behind poor Elena Kolb's homely face!

NOTHING IS EVER REALLY LOST

At ten-thirty he heard Lenora's cane pounding in the hallway.

Then she appeared at the door of his study and asked if he hadn't worked long enough. "It's almost time to go to bed," she said. "Come on, you mad youth, you're tired and don't know it!"

Half protesting, he let her have her way, and began to put things back into his desk and brief case.

She leaned against the door frame and said, "So, have you been reading that girl's journal?"

He nodded.

"Is it interesting?"

"Pretty much the same old thing. More of a personal diary. Very much as anticipated. That's what happens with most of them."

"But isn't that only natural when you're young?" she asked. "Don't you think so?"

"Maybe."

"Is it interesting?"

Then, for some reason he could not have explained, he answered with the protracted feeling that every word he was speaking was half a lie, without his understanding that it *was* a lie, exactly, or how it might have been. "No," he said, "it's pretty much the same old crap."

Lenora nodded sadly and leaned over to put her hand on the arm of his chair.

"How's your leg?" he asked.

"It's all right," she said. "Anyway, I still have one left." The sad old jokes stayed with them, transforming some small part of pain and misery into comfort.

Then, a moment later, she said, "Was she pretty?"

"She chewed gum."

"That doesn't really answer my question."

He nodded. "What I mean is, she was a gum chewer."

"Oh."

"No, she wasn't pretty at all. Nobody could have thought so. She was thick

Moonless Place

and awkward and had jet-black hair that hung down around her face like a...well, it had that slick hard oily texture of a new nylon paint brush."

"You don't often notice the color of women's hair."

"She had the sort you couldn't help but notice."

"Poor girl."

"In a way," he said slowly, feeling ahead as he spoke, "it makes it—now let me say this right—not less *pathetic*, certainly, but somehow less spectacularly sad. I mean, there's a way in which you have to think that maybe...just maybe she didn't have a whole lot to live for. I know you shouldn't think such thoughts as that...but, good God! What am I saying?"

"It's all right," Lenora said.

Hugh nodded. "Because...well, what do you do when you know you shouldn't think something?"

"Think it," Lenora answered dutifully.

"I wouldn't say something like that to anyone else, of course."

"Of course not."

"As I'm always telling my students, you can forget but you can't unremember."

"How can you close your eyes and count to ten without thinking of Dublin?"

"Yes, that's exactly what I tell them."

Lenora said, "We hope God doesn't look at things that way, but we're not God, after all."

"No. We're only human."

"What are those lines you like to quote from Yeats? Something about the girl's beautiful hair..."

"'For only God, my dear, can love you for yourself alone and not your yellow hair.'"

"Yes, that's it."

"Well, something like it, anyway. From all I can remember, she was such a dim, intense, awkward, sentimental girl that you had to wonder why..."

"You're still talking about Elena Kolb?"

"Yes, of course."

"And you were going to say you wonder why *what* ?"

"Not that anyone should ever make such a judgment, of course."

"Of course not," Lenora said, clutching his arm and shaking it with a grip that was so strong it surprised him a little.

Then he noticed that she was still standing, leaning on her cane, while he was propped comfortably in his chair.

But when he mentioned it and started to get up, she shook her head and said, no, it was all right; she was tired of sitting, anyway. Then she seemed to lose herself in thought a moment, gazing off into the distance and pulling her lips in between her teeth in a way she had, suggestive of an almost childish absorption. Finally, she shook her thoughts loose, patted his shoulder, and left his study, saying that Limpy the Clown would wait up for him until he was ready to come to bed.

He said all right, then for some reason once again picked up Elena Kolb's journal and began to leaf through it. Looking for the juicy parts, he would have said if Lenora had been there to hear...saying so ironically, of course, because God knows there *were* no juicy parts. There was very little of anything at all, juicy or otherwise. Elena Kolb might have been just a genderless cog in the machinery, a faceless custodian, a C student in an Introductory Chemistry class.

Thinking of this, he tried to remember what the immediate response of the class had been on the day after her suicide. There were, of course, the obligatory expressions of shock and dismay, but there was nothing in the way of a specific, personal response that he could remember.

And yet, how could anyone expect otherwise? Their student population was big enough that two or three Elena Kolbs might drop out of sight, and if the student newspaper, or the town newspaper, didn't report the fact, nobody would notice at all...except, possibly, for a roommate or the dorm proctor who was obliged to keep records of such things.

Returning to the notebook, he was once again impressed by how unimpressive it was—how drearily predictable, how much like most of the journals handed in for the course. "What exactly is it you want?" was the inevitable question at the beginning of the term; and he would answer: "In your journals you are challenged to ask interesting questions about the world, yourselves, the everyday things around you. There's nothing *intrinsically* devoid of interest, after all. And you're challenged to write about what you think, or about what *might* be thought. Writers have one obligation, and one only: to be interesting in language. They can be ignorant, wrong, silly or strange...but they must be interesting . And there is only one way to be interesting, and that's to be interested . Escape your practical and efficient self, the one you have to be simply to function adequately. Observe this uniquely impractical ceremony for this one moment...at night, perhaps, when you sit down with your journal and preside over the things you will enact as having happened that day—not just "in real life," as we say (hardly knowing what we mean by the expression), but inside your heads—your imaginations, your total sense of what is available to you as a person."

Such instructions were often met with leaden incomprehension, but Hugh

Moonless Place

Devlin was convinced that nothing is really lost, and what the students you are addressing at any particular moment, let us say...what they will miss, and hardly seem to take in at any level, those adults they are destined to become might, in some way, remember and thereby hear. Romantic nonsense, no doubt (he often provided his own most negative response)...and yet, he could feel the presence of those future generations waiting to listen to what he had to say through the intermediation of the sophomores and juniors sitting glazed-eyed in his classes, innocent of that passionate attentiveness he so passionately espoused.

But by the evidence in her diary, no one could accuse this poor dead girl of having been indifferent. She had carried her practical and efficient self with her...except for her being gaga over the idea of being a "poetess"—the only female student he could remember since the advent of Feminist Deconstructionist dogmata who used that certifiably sexist term. She seemed to think of poetry as her vocation, a sort of religious covenant. No doubt her head, like her relentlessly adolescent journal, had been filled with all the clichés of experiencing life poetically. She'd evidently felt about poetry the way most of her peers felt about rock stars and political correctness, trailing all the dusty clichés of liberal social enlightenment as it transvalued traditional values and institutions.

And yet, he couldn't find any evidence in the journal that she had cared about the real thing, or had much of an idea of what the real thing was. Rather, it was the *idea* of poetry (as she would have expressed it), meaning virtually little more than the word itself, along with the rich coloration of its emotional aura. He suspected that there was no conceivable human activity, from incest to cannibalism, that she wouldn't have swooned over if somehow, in her sense of things, the word "poetic" could be attached to it.

Her moony infatuation evidently extended to the person she referred to as "Ernest"—a name almost as old-fashioned in its way as "poetess"; but whoever Ernest was, his name cropped up often, and she seemed to have her private version of a crush on him, casting his image in some dim niche in the wall of her mind's dim cathedral. From her frequent but exasperatingly oblique references, Ernest seemed to be a somewhat remote and self-important figure, a man who evidently lived in a town or city two hundred miles away. One of the references suggested that he might have been her family's Episcopalian minister.

Otherwise, the journal itself was largely unfocused despair and/or inspiration alternating with seizures of "self-expression"—which is to say, a display of chronic self-indulgent feeling. A carnival of thrills and a swirl of emotions that might have been those of a twelve year old. As for that mental life Hugh Devlin challenged his students to attain, however...as for that habitual stripping of the veil of familiarity from the gray mist of daily affairs—she seemed to have been only marginally alive, if the testimony of her journal was valid. In spite of her ardent and frequent attempts to convey the very opposite, the pages were filled only with those sadly muddled cries of pain and ecstasy, familiar notions that were hopelessly conventional, banal, sentimental, and ultimately, alas, trivial.

Once again he laid the notebook down in his lap and stared out the back window of his study. A breeze that was a harbinger of winter tinkled the wind chimes that hung from the patio overhang beyond the screened window. Far over the Detwiler's house, a bank of cumulus clouds was massed as palpable and thick as shaving cream. Upon the faint movement of cold evening air came the distant, compulsive barking of the Wrightmire's neurotic water spaniel, which they kept chained to a post in their back yard so that it could punctuate the long afternoons with its dim-witted barking. No more lawns mowed until next spring.

Hugh shook his head and returned to thoughts of the journal on his lap. Why had her mother insisted that he read it? Could she have somehow thought that *he* was Ernest, for God's sake? Hadn't she realized that her references to that mysterious presence as an older man living two hundred miles away eliminated him? And if not Ernest, what *else* was he supposed to find in it?

But deeper than this, what right had a girl like that poor, feckless, homely, clumsy, plodding, unrewarding creature to kill herself?

POETIC IDEALS

Nevertheless, he dutifully, almost superstitiously, studied every word, especially alert to any hint of personal reference. His failure to alight upon even a single allusion that might explain her mother's odd insistence that he go over the journal made him uneasy. It was almost as if the woman were testing him, teasing him, goading him into betraying a monstrous insensitivity in understanding how this one pathologically sensitive girl had been poised upon the brink of self-annihilation when she wrote things in her diary that were somehow addressed to him, personally.

Of course, from the very beginning, there had been the hint of a suspicion so profoundly disturbing that he scarcely allowed himself to think of it. The dead girl's mother may have seen, or thought she had seen, some evidence that her daughter had committed suicide in a mood of anguished and total despair; and she may have somehow believed that insofar as he, her adored teacher, had destroyed the poor muddled, sentimental, idealistic girl's belief in the possibility of her becoming a poet, Hugh Devlin himself was partly responsible for her self-destruction!

Moonless Place

He understood very well that there were adolescents who killed themselves for sillier reasons. No doubt there were students who killed themselves over something as elemental as grades, as if in failing calculus or Latin one forfeited life itself. Still, it was part of his commitment as a professor of creative writing that such a reason was not necessarily and in itself *silly*, but simply exaggerated. It was merely unbalanced, as we say.

FROM PROF. DEVLIN'S LECTURE ON THE CONFESSIONAL POETS

How insidious it is to be forced into using personal nightmare and fecklessness as the essential subject of poetry. And if you are serious about writing poetry, about "becoming a poet," don't ever come to rely upon pain and suffering as material, for the world will soon expect pain and suffering from you, and if you don't provide it, the world will lose interest.

Surely, this message is clear; and yet, I am aware that your generation is more seriously tempted than others, for the aggrandizement of failure and misery is part of the world you find yourself in. It is part of your value system. But are you aware of the implications? I think not. I think they can be seen only from outside, perhaps from someone in my generation. For example, are you aware of the myth of suffering implicit in your music? Can't you understand what is implied by the hoarse groaning and anguished facial expressions of the rock stars you so much admire? Can't you see beyond those fake gestures and meretricious facades of stylized grief? Don't you know that rock music is emotional masturbation?

What I think of as "your" music exploits and revels in the loss of all rational control—the only sort that can support civilized values. How is this manifest? In the defiant off-key tonality of singers dressed and groomed in the visual rhetoric of barbaric dissent; in the vocal rhetoric of their mispronunciations...exploited by hippy children chanting the substandard English of slaves—for example, mindlessly groaning "mind" to rhyme with the *baa* of sheep as they imitate those speech patterns that were once greater social stigmata than skin color or dress.

The essential message of such tinsel-fake, melodramatic *Angst* is that to be fully alive, you have to live passionately, and to live passionately, you have to be *emotional* and cultivate factitious modes of anguish...which is to say, cultivate an adolescent self-pity articulated by expressions of ostentatiously theatrical suffering. Therefore it is evident, is it not, that along with being hyper-emotional, it is also necessary for a rock star to be somewhat, if not grossly, mentally deficient?

Are these observations, then, also true of those labelled "confessional poets"? I will let you decide whether they are or not.

MISTAKEN IDENTITIES

Lenora seemed withdrawn, of late—saddened by something as nebulous as the light of day, something inaccessible. Several times Hugh looked up from his reading to surprise her in the act of staring at her stiff leg, holding an open book in her lap which she may have been holding without reading a word for God-knows-how long before he happened to glance up and discover her withdrawal into herself.

However his own days were pleasantly cluttered with such minor distractions as committee work and approaching mid-terms. "Troubles come not as single spies," he said in the faculty lounge one day, throwing his arm out in a stylized gesture from 19th century French classical theatre, "but in whole battalions of blue books." No one seemed to think that was funny or even apposite; so he filled his coffee cup in silence, went out into the hallway, and plodded back to his office.

Then, immediately after the bell rang ending his Tuesday Gothic Lit Class, he walked uptown to a local jewelers, where he had left his watch for cleaning and a replacement of the band. He liked the little hole-in-the-wall; he liked the jeweler, who picked up a watch with an expression on his face that seemed to marvel that a mechanism small enough to be worn on the wrist can nevertheless track the rotation of the earth.

He was a fat little man with a thick head of white hair and horn-rimmed glasses, and Hugh had never seen him wearing a tie—always his shirt was open at the neck, and his shirt pocket bristled with a dazzling assortment of gold and silver pens. He must have kept a half-dozen there, which Devlin interpreted as suggesting that in some obscure way if the little fat man were ever seized by inspiration of any sort, he was prepared to sit down and write for days without stopping..."getting it all down in black and white," as his students liked to say in discussing the enthusiastic first drafts of a story or poem.

Today, Hugh had to wait while the little proprietor tended to the needs of a tall saturnine woman dressed in blue suede, with a great puff of pale orange hair and dark eyes haunted by eye shadow. After the proprietor had finished with her and he was fetching his watch from the back room, Devlin turned halfway around to gaze through the large, single front window at the crowds of students passing by...and it was while he was gazing idly upon this current of wildly assorted humanity—fascinating, as always, of course...it was while he was gazing out the front window of the little shop that he saw Elena Kolb walk past.

The shock to him was not entirely like a clap of thunder on a sunny day, but it was what a translation of that into something utterly silent and internal might be. The jeweler was speaking to him, explaining something about the mainspring...but eventually he stopped speaking, probably because of the expression on Devlin's face. In fact, the jeweler himself turned and looked out his front window. But of course, there was nothing for him to see: only a few of the hundreds of students that passed by every day.

"Is anything wrong?" he asked.

"No," Devlin said, shaking his head. "It was just somebody I saw. Or thought I saw. A surprise. It's nothing."

But the expression on his face must have conveyed a different message, and the jeweler did not turn his attention back to the watch he was holding until after another pause.

"It's all right," Devlin said, almost incoherently. "I'll take it."

That was strange enough, as if he were buying the watch instead of merely paying for its repair.

Then, instead of putting it on his wrist, as he would have normally done, he let the jeweler put it in a small puce-colored plastic bag. The little fat man was once again talking about the watch. It was a very good watch, he assured Devlin; it was a quality watch. Swiss made. A watch obviously worth spending money on.

Nodding and paying his bill, Hugh Devlin left the shop, and then started walking swiftly in the direction where the dead girl had been headed. Not that he was likely to overtake her in such a crowd, after such a delay.

But there was no doubt about whom he'd seen: it was the unmistakable image that had occupied his mind so often of late whenever he'd thought of Elena Kolb.

COREEN YARDLEY

Somehow he worked his way through the rest of the day's schedule, even managing to laugh at something said in the lounge while he ate the braunschweiger and cheese sandwich on whole wheat that Lenora had made for him. While others talked, he sipped cold apple juice from his thermos and then dutifully ate a raw carrot. Some of his colleagues had fixed up a dart board and kept score on a sheet of paper pinned on the wall beside it. A bit of cozy old England surviving from their sabbaticals.

When the talk ceased momentarily, he could hear the plunk of darts as one of them—Tichnor, probably—eased his long frame forward and flung away at the target board, now shredded to the color and soft texture of leftover yams, with the target lines scarcely visible.

Thinking vaguely of this, Devlin felt something obscure stir deep down in the darkness of his memory. Something about Elena Kolb. He closed his eyes for a moment and concentrated upon his memory of that scene from the jeweler's shop: the girl striding swiftly past, wearing a loose shirt over walking shorts, the straight oily black hair bouncing with her stride...and then the bewildering miscellaneousness of other students hurrying past in both directions.

Devlin stood up and was surprised to find that he was shaking his head. Tichnor, who'd stopped popping his darts, asked if something was the matter.

"Oh, just classes," he muttered.

"Yeah, it gets like that this time of year," Vogel agreed.

Devlin said something generally appropriate, and then walked out of the lounge. He went back to his office and got out the roll book. He turned to Elena Kolb's name and saw that it had been crossed out with the date November 2 behind it. Then he ran his finger down the list until he came to the name of Coreen Yardley. It, also, had been crossed out; and behind it was the date, November 5. That would have been the day when he'd signed the drop slip. He saw that she had missed several classes in a row before that.

He closed his eyes and thought. Then he opened them and—though no one was there to see, and he was perfectly aware of what he was doing—he nodded. The two girls had left his class at virtually the same time, one presumably going to another class, the other to her death. The girl he'd remembered as Elena Kolb was the girl he'd seen today; but she was Coreen Yardley, not Elena Kolb at all.

Then he remembered her. Of course! How could he have possibly confused the two? It was suddenly all very clear to him. Elena Kolb had been a thin, haunted-looking girl—pale and blonde, with a delicate oval face and small white hands that she had clasped in her lap while he called the roll.

Exactly the tense, withdrawn fey sort of girl who would be likely to kill herself.

And thinking this, all that he knew about Elena Kolb was suddenly, miraculously, transformed. Everything was subtly, almost magically changed by his realization of who it was that had really written that journal...precisely as the same words spoken by different people can take on radically different meanings.

It was all terribly unfair, and a little bit eerie; but it did make a difference, after all.

Moonless Place

HUGH EXPLAINS HIS ERROR TO LENORA

When he got out of his car at the end of the driveway, he saw that Lenora was standing at the back of the lawn, facing away from him—apparently gazing down at their flower borders. Wearing pale blue slacks and a crisp white blouse, she was leaning hard on her cane, and her head was lowered in an attitude suggestive of profound meditation, or perhaps intense scrutiny.

Evidently, she hadn't heard him drive up. So he walked back softly through the grass, hoping to surprise her. But she heard him and turned around when he was still some twenty feet away. The expression on her face shocked him, for it was obvious she had been crying. She managed a sudden, bright, instantaneous smile; but there was something so desperate and brave in the attempt, he didn't have the heart to break the seal of her pretense and ask what was wrong.

"Well, this is a nice surprise," she said, managing to swing her cane almost jauntily. "You're home early."

"I've shed enough light for one day," he said. Another sad old joke, but, like all those others, comfortable for that very reason.

"I'll see about dinner, then. Do you feel like eating early?"

"Sure. Any time."

They walked together back to the kitchen, and when they entered the coolness of the house, Lenora said, "I've been wondering—did that poor dead girl's mother ever get back to you?"

Hugh shook his head and frowned. "No, I haven't heard a thing from her."

Lenora braced her cane against the edge of the sink and counter, then pivoted on one foot so she could reach into the refrigerator.

"How's the leg been today?" he asked.

"I wish you wouldn't ask me that!" she whispered.

He held his open hands out to the side in a gesture of helplessness. "I only wanted to know if it was bothering you."

She inhaled sharply and then her face softened. "I know. I shouldn't have snapped at you. It's all right. Pretty much the same, I guess."

Hugh sat down in one of the kitchen chairs and miserably dropped his forehead into his hand. After a moment, he said. "I have something to tell you. It's not important, but…"

"Of course it's important," she said when he paused. "I'm sure it must be."

Hugh nodded. "Do you remember that time when you asked me what Elena Kolb looked like?"

She turned from the sink and looked at him. "Yes?"

He ran his hand through his hair and dropped it heavily on the table. "Well, I found out I was thinking of the wrong one."

"What do you mean, the wrong one?"

He nodded. "There was another girl, Coreen Yardley, who dropped out of the class about the same time as Elena Kolb killed herself. I got the two of them mixed up in my memory. I saw her today, as big as life. And it gave me quite a jolt. I mean, I was sure the Yardley girl was Elena Kolb."

"She was the one with the black hair that hung down like...what was it you said? A new nylon paint brush."

"Yes. And it's still hanging down like that."

"It must have been a shock, seeing her like that."

He nodded. "Yes, it was."

After a moment's silence, Lenora said, "What did the dead girl look like, then?"

Hugh smiled wistfully. "The *real* dead girl...well, she was thin and pale. Skinny, almost. And a little bit out of it, I guess you'd say."

"Did she have light hair?"

Hugh nodded again. "Yes, she was a blonde. Very delicate features."

"It sounds as if she might have been beautiful," Lenora said, turning back to the sink.

"I think you could say that," Hugh admitted judiciously. "But from what her mother told me, there must have been something terribly wrong with her. Mentally."

"Isn't that more or less implicit in the fact that she killed herself?"

"Of course, only...well, I'm not so sure we can assume that anyone who commits suicide is mentally deranged."

"Sure. As in, who's to define normality."

"Something like that. Of course you had to make such an assumption in your practice, just to operate."

Lenora nodded. "Yes, it was one of the assumptions. Actually more of an axiom, I guess you'd say."

"Essential, no doubt."

"The point is, I don't think that anyone who cancels everything, for *good*, as they say, can be rational. Let's just say that suicide's not healthy. That's a modest-enough premise. It limits your options."

"Unless they've been forced into an irrational circumstance, of some sort."

"Perhaps."

"And I suppose that if you learned enough about her, none of it would be surprising, would it?"

"To know all is to forgive all."

Hugh nodded. "Well, something like that, too, I suppose."

ELENA'S PHOTO

The next day, he went over to the registrar's office in Clendennin Hall, also known as the Administration Building. It was a tall, ungainly architectural dinosaur that frowned over the campus oval out of cathedral windows deep-set in rough old hand-made brick the color of old dried blood. Clendennin was one of the Gothic structures he had mentioned in his lecture.

He walked up the stairs to the second floor, where the Student Records offices were, and asked for the I.D. card of Elena Kolb. The woman behind the desk was warmly fat with a wide pleasant face. He told her Elena was deceased. He said she had been his student, and he needed to verify something in her record.

She excused herself and went into the records section, returning a moment later to hand him a student I.D. card with Elena Kolb's photograph on it. He thanked her and held the card in both hands and studied it a moment. The image seemed to stare out at him from a distance so great that her face loomed almost out of focus. He took another long breath as he contemplated the slightly mussed appearance of a girl just awakened from a deep sleep.

All of which was fanciful, of course; and he told himself as much as he handed the picture back to the woman.

"I remember reading about her suicide," the woman said. "It certainly was a shame, wasn't it?"

"Yes," Hugh muttered, "it certainly was." His voice hadn't sounded right, so he cleared his throat. But instead of repeating what he'd said, he merely nodded and walked out of the records office without even thanking her.

When he returned to his own office, he once again picked up Elena Kolb's journal and began to read it. By now, he could almost repeat some of the words *verbatim*; and yet they would never be quite the same as when he'd thought Coreen Yardley had written them. It was not just, nor was it sensible, that this should be so; but there was no arguing with what he heard and felt as he now gazed at the familiar text.

But the central mystery remained: exactly why had the dead girl's mother left the journal with him? And having done so, why hadn't she gotten back in touch? There was something odd, almost ominous, about it; and during the past few weeks, he had occasionally paused from reading or marking a paper, and looked

Moonless Place

over to see Elena's notebook lying there on top of the filing cabinet, radiating its woeful mediocrity upon everything around it. And yet, he could not escape the idea that there was something in it he hadn't quite grasped—something mysterious, therefore *not* mediocre...perhaps something for him alone. Why else had her mother been so oddly insistent? And what was it the girl's mother might understand that he couldn't? "In a way," she had said, "Elena's diary is addressed to *you*."

Going over papers only the day before, he had found the thought of the journal darkening his mind, so that he eventually sighed, tossed his grading pencil aside, stood up, went over to the notebook and picked it up. He opened it at random and stared at the entry for October 15th. Then he turned several leaves and began to read from a passage that caused him to pause and think. A very small, but very surprising realization came over him: perhaps her mother hadn't been entirely wrong; maybe there had been "something there" after all, which had for some reason surfaced in this single entry:

> April 28: I remember seeing three students talking together with their heads almost touching. They were two guys and a girl. They acted like they didn't know anybody else was around. How can people be so obsessed this way? How can they get lost in gossip when there are so many really important issues in the world at large? How easily we lose our perspective on things and let our petty affairs absorb us. I hate the small gossip that buzzes all around. I guess I always have and always will. Oh, well! There are other things to concern oneself with. We all have our own life to live. I should be above such things and accept loneliness, if I can lay claim to be above anything. But sometimes I wonder if I can. Sometimes I wonder if my poetry will ever be appreciated. <u>It means so much to me</u>! Sometimes I could just cry out from it, as if it were a small baby inside, crying out to be born, as if it knows something beautiful already and wants to join the world.

"Join the world," Hugh whispered, savoring the odd sense of the words as they swam to the surface out of the depths of so much murk.

Moonless Place

THE BEE-BEE SYNDROME

Then, late that night in his study at home, he read another entry:

> When I think of what it must be to be born to be a poet, I shudder at the terrific responsibility. What must it be to be published and have one's words remain alive after one is gone, words set forever in type to be there for everybody in the whole world to read, so that there will be no hiding from that time on? Everyone must feel this way, for everyone is a poet at heart, no matter how little he or she may realize the fact. I wonder what sort of poetry Ernest writes.

This passage suffered splendidly from what Devlin called "The Bee-Bee Syndrome," insisting that a student guilty of such stylistic befuddlement read it aloud, but otherwise refusing to explain what he meant by the term. And when the student complied and read it aloud, the coin would almost always drop.

But would it have dropped in *her* head? Had the assignments Elena Kolb handed in been as cumbersome as her journal? If so, had Hugh asked her to read anything aloud in class...in which case had the girl been humiliated or had she even comprehended? Could she, for instance, have understood how dead was her reference to words that "remain alive after one is gone"?

Unable to remember, Hugh shook his head. Then he looked at the passage again and contemplated the fact that in a strange way Elena had finally managed through her suicide to draw the most painfully aware attention to something she'd written, thus claiming for herself the sort of privilege that in her own scheme of things was the greatest possible privilege of all—to have one's words judged as poetry.

Hugh thought of the cult of suffering, at least as old as the romantics, but with its wailing and moaning still echoing in the modern canon, deconstructed or not. He had often scorned the premise of confessional poetry, telling his undergraduates that it was a perilous truth for sophomores—which was doubly relevant, for in a way, all poets were sophomores. He told them he was trusting them in articulating such an idea; but he knew it wasn't all trust, for part of him cynically relied upon their opacity or intellectual laziness to mitigate whatever harm it might work in their imaginations. And yet, was it conceivable that just this one time it had taken root in the frenetic imagination of a fey teeny-bopper who had somehow fastened upon the idea of becoming a poet?

Then, too, he could not finally avoid dwelling upon the irony of how that confused, passionate, untalented girl had now through her own words achieved something very much like what she had yearned to achieve—not by writing unforgettable poetry, but by committing the unforgettable, unforgivable and unanswerable act of killing herself halfway through the fall term, without preamble or warning.

And yet, could he be sure there had not been a sign? Had she in some way called out for help? Wasn't that possibility implicit in her mother's melodramatic insistence that he read her journal? And wasn't it possible that in the portion he'd read there'd been some clue he'd ignored, a clue he should have seized upon with the realization that in her own muddled way Elena Kolb was crying out for help, but he had proved too insensitive, too preoccupied, too self-absorbed, too glibly articulate to hear?

Suddenly he looked up to see Lenora standing in the doorway of his study. Looking tired, she asked if he wasn't tired, too. He removed his glasses and closed his eyes, saying, yes, he was very tired.

"Then why don't we go to bed?" Lenora said.

"I think that's a very wise decision," Hugh muttered.

When he awoke that night, he thought about the journal and it suddenly came to him that what her entries were about was time —which, as he had often told his students, was the secret subject of so much of what we are thinking about when we are not aware that we are thinking about time.

FROM PROF. DEVLIN'S LECTURE ON THE SEMANTICS OF THE PSEUDONYM

What, precisely, is the rhetorical effect of signing one's name to a poem or story? If you know you were going to put another person's name to what you write, does this affect how you write it? How significantly do pseudonyms alter whatever is written? What motivates authors to put another name to a text they've personally created? And yet, isn't all writing "putting on another name"? Because when you sign your name to a poem or story, aren't you using that name in a way that is mysteriously different from all its other uses, therefore unique? Is it possible that different labels do not alter the reference?

WHERE IN YOUR LIFE WOULD YOU BE HAPPY, AND WHERE MISERABLE?

On Saturday, Lenora was depressed, and Hugh said he thought it was caused by the cold dark weather. Lenora agreed, but the truth didn't help. And of course they both knew there was something else, entirely unrelated to the weather; for she had been brooding over recent news that one of her sorority sisters from long ago had just died of cancer. Lenora and she had once been very close; although they had not been in touch for years. But then, two nights ago, she had gotten a phone call with the unexpected news of her death.

After dinner, Lenora poured coffee for the two of them, and when she'd settled down, she said, "We keep thinking we're going to go somewhere in life and do something *conclusive*, don't we? Only it doesn't really ever happen that way, does it?"

"No," Hugh said. "Not really."

"We have trouble learning the right things to expect from life. Don't you suppose?"

Then, almost irrelevantly, Hugh asked her a question he sometimes asked his students: "If by some kind of magic you had the power to determine your own fate... would you choose to live a life of sustained desperation and misery, then die transfigured by joy... or live a happy and even joyful life up to the very end... but then die in utter and terrible despair?"

The calm slow perplexity of Lenora's gaze made him uneasy and he began to explain. "You see, whichever answer they give... I ask them why they chose *that* answer."

"I see. And why do they?"

"Different reasons, of course. But always interesting, I think. Whatever they say reveals something about themselves."

Lenora smiled slowly and shook her head. "As long as we've been married, I've never gotten used to the odd ideas you come up with. And questions."

He nodded earnestly. "Of course it seems odd; but there's a point to it, after all."

"Oh, I'm sure. There always is."

"Some of them refuse to answer. Do you know why?"

"No, why?"

"Well, I think it's a form of superstition. A kind of reluctance to answer such a question."

"I can understand that."

"Because it's *tabu* to preside over something as profound and majestic as... as deciding your own fate, for God's sake!"

"Although we do it all the time, in little ways."

"Yes, but doesn't that make all the difference? Because it's always imperfectly, and always in little ways. We couldn't get along, we couldn't get from one thing to the next if we didn't choose our fates in *little* ways."

"But what about your students?"

"After they give their answers, I tell them that there is no answer to such a question."

"I think," Lenora said thoughtfully, "that might be because it doesn't really give you anything to grab onto."

"BeeBee," Hugh said.

"Oh, did I do that? Yes, I guess I did. I said, 'be because.' Well, well."

"Never mind. It doesn't make any difference. I've been grading too many papers."

"But don't you agree?" Lenora asked him. "That there's nothing to grab onto with a question like that?"

Hugh grabbed the bridge of his nose with thumb and finger. "No, I think it challenges us to visit places we haven't visited."

"I assume you're talking about ideas."

"Yes. I think it challenges us to look at certain values and expectations in a different way."

"Maybe."

"But of course the point is that nobody with any sense would ever, ever make such a choice."

Lenora smiled. "*I* certainly wouldn't."

"So if there's a correct answer—which is to say, a shrewd one, or a wise one, it's the answer of those who refuse to play the game at all."

"*Tabu*," Lenora said.

"And yet, just for a moment the question asks us to consider this distinction, a distinction that says something about us and where we place our values."

"Where we place them in *time*, you mean."

"Yes, but in other ways, as well. For example, choosing a miserable life with an exalted and perhaps even apocalyptic ending is based upon the idea that our lives are essentially dramatic. We like a good ending."

"Well, if it fits, we certainly do."

"Good point. But also that they're like accounts. So that through years of

Moonless Place

suffering and misery..."

Lenora interrupted: "You're accumulating credit and paying for a happy ending."

"Exactly. While doing it the other way, you're revealing that it's the present moment that counts, and not only that, it's the amount of time you're happy. Forty years of happiness can be a bargain if you weigh it against a few hours or weeks of fear and despair at the end."

"It's like going into debt, then."

"Precisely."

"And all that time you're happy—every day and every hour—you're accumulating more and more debt, and you've got that horror waiting for you."

"Sure, but if you don't know..."

"Yes, and that's why the choice itself is *tabu*. The question is really dividing people into grasshoppers and ants, isn't it?"

"Well, in a way I suppose the distinction is as old as Aesop."

"But in the one scenario... I'm not exactly sure whether you're talking about *illumination* at the end of life, or *ecstasy*."

For a moment, Hugh pondered. "Well, I'm not sure either."

Lenora smiled. "And it's your question!"

"I guess I was just thinking of it as a semantic package in which neither would be possible without the other."

"I see."

"But of course there's only one healthy response to a question like that, and that's to ask for both. Happiness throughout, then dying in a state of ecstasy and grace."

"That would be my preference, certainly."

"And yet, I can't help but think that the question has a certain interest and importance."

"Do your students think so?"

"I *think* they think so. But something like that is always hard for me to judge."

For a moment, they fell silent. Hugh sipped his coffee and Lenora studied her thumbnail. Finally she said, "And which would you choose, if you couldn't have both?"

"I have no idea," Hugh admitted.

"Well, then," Lenora sighed, "I guess that makes two of us."

That night Hugh awoke and had trouble going back to sleep. His head was lazily busy with a variety of images and memories, but a sudden question came to him: did Elena Kolb's life somehow fit that equation? Had she experienced her version of sustained ecstasy in her vision of becoming a poet, and then perhaps realizing that she had no gift for it at all, had she fallen into such utter despair that she killed herself by taking an overdose of sleeping tablets while she was alone in the dormitory one Saturday night?

But that didn't exactly fit the question; and Hugh knew it didn't, because, for one thing, it could have been the other way around.

LENORA'S HOPE

By next spring, Lenora's leg had gotten so much worse, her doctor arranged for a new two-day treatment at the Brander Falls Clinic only two hundred miles to the north.

"They'll probably want me to stay over," Lenora told Hugh.

"Then we'll stay over."

"And there's something else I thought of."

"What?"

"Well, there's no point in your just sitting there waiting for me and reading."

"There's nothing I like better."

Lenora nodded. "I know. But I was just thinking, wasn't that poor girl from Pemberton?"

"Pemberton?"

"Yes, Pemberton. And isn't Pemberton near Brander Falls?"

"Well, it's about the same distance. To the east of Brander Falls; but not very far."

"How far?"

"I'm not sure. I'd have to look at a map."

"Come on! You have an idea, don't you?"

"Well, I don't suppose it's over thirty or forty miles."

"That's just what I thought," Lenora said, nodding with a look of determined satisfaction on her face.

"*What's* what you thought?"

"I think you should make a point of going to see her."

"See whom?"

"Hugh, don't be dense. I'm talking about the dead girl's mother, of course. I find it so strange what she asked of you. I'm talking about that business of the diary, of course."

"Journal."

"Journal, then. And the fact that she's never gotten back in touch with you

Moonless Place

or anything. And you haven't called her."

"Yes."

"I think with something like that, you should really, you know, sit down and talk with her, and find out exactly what it was she had in mind. Don't you?"

"Well, I'm not sure."

"Of course you should!" Then Lenora took a long deep breath and said, "Don't think I haven't noticed how much it's bothered you."

"Yes, it's bothered me, all right."

"Don't think I haven't noticed," Lenora repeated.

DEVLIN ARRANGES TO HAVE LUNCH WITH MRS. KOLB

When Hugh phoned, his approach was matter-of-fact and businesslike. After introducing himself, he said, "Mrs. Kolb, my wife will be in the Brander Falls Clinic on Wednesday, the twenty-fourth, and I'm wondering if I might come to Pemberton that day and talk with you."

"Brander Falls?"

"Yes. It's only thirty-five miles away."

"Yes, I know where it is."

"Perhaps you'll be my guest for lunch, if you could recommend some place."

There was a pause, and Mrs. Kolb said, "Exactly what is this all about, Professor Devlin?"

"It's about Elena's journal."

"I see."

"Mrs. Kolb, you were very emphatic about wanting me to read it."

"Yes, I suppose I was, at that."

"And I've never quite understood why."

"I see."

"I've found it all very perplexing."

"Perplexing," she repeated. "So you want to talk to me about it. Is that right?"

"Exactly. I've given it my careful attention, Mrs. Kolb. And time. Then, too, I was expecting you to get back to me."

"I see."

"So do you suppose we could meet for lunch?"

After the briefest pause, she said, "Well, let me think. Wednesday, the twenty-fourth, you say. Yes, that would be all right, I suppose."

"Good. Where would you suggest?"

"Well, the Brander Falls Country Club would be nice. Although it's very expensive."

"That's all right."

"Well, then, it's on Georgetown Pike, not very far from the I-89 turn-off."

"Let me write that down."

"The Brander Falls Country Club."

"All right. On Georgetown Pike, near the I 89 turn-off. I'm sure I can find it. Shall we say noon?"

"Yes, noon will be all right."

After he hung up, Lenora said, "What did she say?"

"She said it will be all right."

"And you'll take her to lunch?"

"Yes. At the Brander Falls Country Club."

"Good," Lenora said. "I've heard of it. It's very exclusive."

"I'm sure we can afford it."

"I'm dying to hear her explanation."

"I am too," Hugh said. "I only hope she has one."

"Why of course, she has one. She'd *have* to, wouldn't she?"

"One would think so," Hugh said. "But, of course, one can never be sure."

AT THE BRANDER FALLS COUNTRY CLUB

At 12:05, Hugh greeted Mrs. Kolb in the dining room's lobby. She was splendidly dressed in a pale green dress with dark green appointments. Lenora would have appreciated every detail.

When they were seated, Mrs. Kolb asked about his wife.

Hugh said, "Everything's going well, and we're hopeful about the new treatment."

"I hope it's successful."

Something in her voice prompted him to continue. "I won't be able to see her until four o'clock at the earliest. And since I couldn't have been with her at all, why ..."

"Of course," Mrs. Kolb repeated, though suggesting something quite different.

The waitress came and they both ordered the special, a gazpacho and tossed salad with cornbread muffins. Hugh suggested a half-carafe of Rosé and Mrs. Kolb agreed.

When the waitress left, Hugh said, "I'm not sure it's necessary, but I don't know your first name."

Moonless Place

Flustered, Mrs. Kolb said, "Oh, I'm sorry. It's Sylvia. Maid of the Forest."

"Yes," Hugh said. "And I'm Hugh. Not 'Professor Devlin,' please."

For a moment neither said anything, then Hugh cleared his throat and said, "I think I mentioned why I wanted to talk with you."

"Of course. You wanted to know why I thought it was so important for you to read Elena's journal. Is that right?"

"Yes."

"I was hoping that when you read it you'd see what I meant."

"You were testing me?"

"Well, in a way, I suppose I was. Only...well, if I'd prompted you in some way, it wouldn't have been the same, would it?"

"No, but the fact is, I didn't find anything."

Sylvia Kolb nodded. "I'm sorry. And yet I had to consider the possibility that I was imagining it."

"That's all right," Hugh said. "Obviously you're talking about some sort of latent text, then."

Uncomfortably, Sylvia nodded. "You make it sound like an academic exercise."

"Like testing someone?"

"*Touché*, Professor Devlin."

"So there was something there that you felt was important, but you weren't sure it was there. And this had something to do with Elena, of course—as it must have done, since she'd written it; but also, you said, it concerned me."

Sylvia nodded without looking at him. "You were very important to her."

"I see," Hugh said, clearing his throat nervously. "And yet...and yet it's hard for me to imagine that there could have been something like a...well, some kind of sexual attraction of any sort."

She looked up. "What?"

"Mrs. Kolb, I am a middle-aged man. I suffer from no illusion that I'm attractive to women. Or girls. I know there are women who are attracted to certain men because they're homely, but...And I've been told that there are women who are somewhat attracted by my voice and the way I speak, and don't think I haven't cultivated it! Have you ever heard the story about John Wilkes, who had a radical strabismus, but boasted that when he met a woman he could 'talk his squint away in half an hour.'"

"Professor Devlin, I don't think that..." She paused to make a small gesture of hopelessness.

"Not only that, I am as monogamous as any man you could name."

He suddenly looked hard at her, and seeing that Sylvia's face had turned red, he threw himself into the nearest available association. "Perhaps you've heard the old rhyme that goes:

>Hoggamus, higgamus,
>men are polygamous;
>Higgamus, Hoggamus,
>women monogamous.

Well, it's an amusing rhyme, but it is only a rhyme, after all. And the fact is, there are many, many quite normal, quite vigorously masculine men who are as monogamous as I am. Also, I hope it isn't hopelessly smug of me to say that in every important way, my wife and I are blessed with a wonderful, wonderful marriage!"

Seeing her look, he added, "Relationship," as if she might need a translation. Then he picked up his water glass and gulped half of it down, sensing that something was suddenly and terribly wrong. And indeed something was, for he'd intended to take a sip of wine, instead of gulping down half the glass of water.

Then with her eyes lowered, Sylvia nodded and said, "I think maybe I've given you the wrong impression."

"These are deep waters, after all."

"*What* are? I don't understand!"

"Sylvia...I think it would be egotistical and presumptive of me to read into Elena's diary what you are suggesting!"

Suddenly agitated, Mrs. Kolb clawed the air with both hands. "*Suggesting*? Why, I wasn't suggesting *that*, for God's sake! It was something entirely different."

He opened his eyes. "Well, I...I was sure it wasn't anything, you know, *romantic*, or anything."

"Oh, of course not! How...how grotesque ."

"Exactly what I was trying to tell you, only..."

There was a moment's silence when he gazed upon his wine glass as he twirled it by the stem.

She cleared her throat. "That really is a terrible stereotype, you know."

He looked up. "What is?"

Sylvia made a face. "That young girls are always romantic. That all they think about is *romance*."

"I've always insisted upon contradistinguishing diaries from journals," Hugh said, gazing at the half-empty half-carafe of wine. Suddenly, he snatched it up and began to pour Rosé in her glass.

Moonless Place

"No more for me, thank you," she said primly.

He nodded and refilled his own wine glass. Then he looked at his water glass and drank the rest of his water. "I hope my wife's all right."

"Why, I hope so too," Mrs. Kolb murmured, sounding surprised.

"She suffers a great deal."

"Oh, I know how painful arthritis can be. My mother suffered from it terribly."

"Terribly," Hugh echoed. Then he drank down the rest of his wine.

Stunned, he sat there for a quiet moment, almost fancying that he could hear waves slapping against the pier. "What is it, then? Or what was it?"

"What it was...what it was," Mrs. Kolb whispered, "Elena looked upon you as a *father!*"

Was, was echoed somewhere in the depths of Hugh's brain. "I see," he finally managed to mutter in a hoarse voice. He cleared his throat and spoke a little louder. "I see."

"Don't you see?" Sylvia Kolb asked, clutching her fingers before her chin. "Years ago when Elena's father and I were divorced, she was only eleven years old, and she missed him so terribly, so terribly...and then when she was in your class and listened to your way of speaking, and your calm manner and everything...shortly after she'd enrolled in your class she just raved about you in her diary. Surely, you picked up on it!"

"No," Hugh said, running his hand through his hair, "I can't really say I did."

"Didn't you know you were Ernest," she whispered.

"The importance of being," he muttered at his wine glass. "Or perhaps Hemingway. In either case, it's impossible."

She nodded, as if agreeing with him. But she wasn't agreeing at all. "I was sure you would notice."

"Why should I notice, when it's utterly absurd?"

She shook her head. "I don't think so."

"For one thing, this *Ernest* she wrote about obviously lived out of town. Somewhere else. Two hundred miles away, in fact. She said so."

"Well, didn't you 'live out of town' so far as she was concerned?"

"Of *course* not! Unless..."

"Her home was in Pemberton, after all."

He frowned. "But surely she wouldn't have thought of where we were all living as being 'out of town'!"

"Being away at the university is always temporary for students."

Hugh sipped some more wine. "Nevertheless...nevertheless, that doesn't prove anything !"

"'Prove'?" she echoed. "What does *proof* have to do with it?"

Hugh drank from his wine glass. "Do with what?"

Sylvia Kolb shook her head sadly. "This isn't a *murder* investigation, Professor Devlin!"

"I didn't think it was."

"Well, then, why do you speak of something like *proof*?"

"Because..."

"I'm sorry to interrupt, but there's something else you didn't notice. All of her references to 'Ernest' were to someone who's older and wiser, a person of authority."

"That still doesn't mean anything. It was a pseudonym. For some reason, she didn't refer to him by his real name because...well, for any of a dozen reasons."

"Do you know the name of my ex-husband? It's Ernie Kolb. Ernest was her father's name."

"Well, then, that's who it was!"

"No, because she would never have called her father by his first name. And it doesn't fit in other ways. She referred to him as someone she was seeing more or less regularly and listening to. She wrote things like...like, 'I wonder what Ernest will say' about this or that."

Hugh closed his eyes and took a deep breath.

"And I have to tell you something else."

He opened his eyes. "Yes?"

"You look very much like her father. The resemblance is quite striking. I noticed it the first time we met. I can remember just sitting there in your office and not being able to say a word, practically, because of how much you reminded me of Ernie. Of course, you couldn't be expected to know that, but I was hoping that when you reread her journal, especially after what happened..."

Hugh grunted and once again ran his hand through his hair.

She tapped the tablecloth with her fingernail. "The instant I saw you, I realized that...well, *something* of what you must have meant to her."

After a moment, Hugh said, "Why on earth didn't you get back in touch with me?"

Slowly Sylvia Kolb blinked. "After I came to see you, I began to wonder if I was right, after all. But not now, not after seeing you again. Also, I began to wonder if I had the right to meddle in your life like this."

"Like this," Hugh echoed.

"Yes. Like this. But when I saw you today, I realized exactly how she must

Moonless Place

have felt about you!"

"I see. You felt it."

For a moment she was silent, then she swallowed and said, "I can see that it was all a mistake. I shouldn't have agreed to meet with you. I can see you're hurt or offended, somehow. And I'm sorry for that. Only, to tell you the truth, Professor Devlin, your grief doesn't seem like much against the life of my beautiful young daughter who killed herself."

"No," Hugh Devlin said in a hollow voice, "I'm sure it doesn't."

The waiter brought their check and Hugh put his hand over it as if it were the hand of someone in need of calm reassurance.

"Do you know what she admired most about you?"

"My voice?" Hugh asked.

"Well, next to your voice."

"No, what?"

"She admired your maturity."

Hugh shook his head and looked up at the ceiling. "What does that mean, exactly?"

"Do your remember the entry where she mentions how all the students show off and try to impress their professor and one another, and at that very moment she suddenly realized something about Ernest. Do you know what?"

"His maturity."

Sylvia nodded. "Yes, his maturity. She said that right then she realized that Ernest was content *not to write*, which is to say, he could look down upon all of them striving to be brilliant and create great literature and so forth, and he wasn't touched by it at all. I think she used the word 'Olympian.'"

"Yes, she did. I remember."

Then, for a long moment he was silent. Finally, he looked at her and said, "Remarkable."

"Yes, isn't it?"

"Remarkable that such a young girl could have such perceptions."

"She *was* remarkable, Professor Devlin!"

For a moment they were both silent. Then he gathered courage to look at the extraordinary woman across from him, as she took a mirror from her purse and frowned into it. "Oh, dear!" she said. "I'm going to have to go to the powder room. Will you excuse me?"

Hugh said of course he would. Then he stood and watched her walk away. When he sat back down, he folded his hands beside his plate and stared at them. Something classical was playing sedately in the background, and he listened to it half-heartedly, trying to recognize it. But he couldn't; and at the moment, he felt he couldn't recognize anything or do anything right. Certainly, at the moment he felt incapable of understanding anything.

When she returned, he paid the bill and escorted her out to the parking lot, down a line of cars until he came to hers, a slightly aged, dusty tan Mercedes with a dented rear fender.

When she unlocked the door, he held it open for her and said, "It's all very mysterious, isn't it?"

"Yes," she said, before sliding in, "it is."

"And I don't suppose anyone knows why, do they?"

"Why what?"

"Why she did it?"

"Well, I'm sure that's the general feeling. But as sad as it is, there's no mystery if you know the facts."

"What facts?"

Sylvia Kolb swallowed. "Elena suffered from depression all her life. She'd tried to kill herself in high school. As it is, she died younger than Keats."

"My God!" Hugh whispered. "I didn't see anything like that in her journal."

"No, it wasn't in her journal."

"So she must have been very secretive, after all," Hugh said.

"Isn't everyone?" Sylvia Kolb asked.

"And disciplined," Hugh said.

"Oh, yes. She was disciplined, all right. I think she knew exactly what had to be done, every day of her life. Right up to the end."

He shook his head. "I don't think I've ever known anyone like that."

"No, I don't think I have, either. But knowing that, of course, it wasn't the same."

"You mean her killing herself."

Sylvia nodded. "In spite of the terrible, terrible sadness—and the horror—I found something like dignity in the way she took things into her own hands."

"Yes, I can see how that would be possible."

Mrs. Kolb turned on the ignition and started the car. Hugh took his hand away. "But as sad as it is, we have to keep on living. All of us."

She hesitated a moment, then said, "I'm going to be married in the fall, you know."

"No, I didn't know. Best wishes."

Sylvia smiled. "Thank you, Professor Devlin. And good luck to you. I hope your wife is all right."

He nodded. "Yes, I think she'll be all right."

Then he watched as Sylvia Kolb drove slowly out of the parking lot of the Brander Falls Country Club, the right turn signal of her Mercedes winking as she pulled out into the right lane of the Georgetown Pike.

DRIVING HOME FROM THE BRANDER FALLS CLINIC

Lenora's two-day treatment at the Brander Falls Clinic was judged a success, which meant that she emerged with less pain than she had entered. The treatment would have to be repeated at intervals, and no one had ever spoken of it as a cure; but in the nature of things, it was a welcome change in what Hugh and she had begun to think of as an inevitable decline in her condition.

Returning home the following evening, they drove with the air conditioning and radio on, keeping out the shimmering heat and silence. They stopped for dinner at a small town hotel restaurant, advertised as a "family restaurant" which Hugh said meant no wine or booze, and Lenora said that was all right. And when they parked, Lenora decided to walk in without her cane. "I feel liberated," she said, when they reached the front door.

They were shown to a table next to a large window, where they could watch several swans moving in and out of a small pond bordered by shrubs and swings for children. Because of the heat, the shrubs were turning a pale brown, and the swings hung as empty as nooses from a scaffold. Heat had affected everything; even the swans seemed to move reluctantly in an inscrutable slow-motion choreography.

When the waitress refilled their tall, frosted iced tea glasses, Lenora said, "I keep thinking of what you've told me about your conversation with her."

"I found it all very strange," Hugh said.

"Certainly you don't blame her for getting married again, do you?"

"No, of course not. Although it seemed odd to hear of it like that, right before she roared away in her car."

"She didn't actually *roar* away, did she?"

Hugh smiled. "No, she didn't roar away. In fact, she made a very sedate exit. Still, having just tossed off that last bit of information about getting married, almost as an afterthought..."

"Life must go on, as they say."

"Yes, they do say that."

Lenora sipped at her iced tea. "But at least you found out what you wanted to know. At least you found out why she'd wanted you to read the diary."

Hugh nodded. "Yes, strange as it was."

"And that was all of it? She just wanted you to understand that you had become a man named Ernest, who was both her father and yet not her father."

"That seemed to be all of it. But learning now about it...knowing she was about to *die*, that she looked upon me that way!"

Lenora shivered eloquently. "Yes, that's the part that's so strange. And moving, somehow."

"And the instant she said it, I thought: 'What an extraordinary girl!'"

"Indeed she was. If, that is..."

"Yes? If what?"

Lenora shook her head rapidly. "If what she said is true."

"I know," Hugh said. "I've wondered the same thing. And yet, why would her own mother *lie* about such a thing?"

Lenora folded her hands in her lap. "I know, I know."

"But I confess that it sounded melodramatic, the way she told me. Somehow, it almost sounded as if she didn't quite believe it herself. Or just wanted it to be said."

"I don't think we have any way of knowing," Lenora said.

"Which means, life has to go on for us, too."

"I would hope so."

"Still, you'd think that her own mother..."

"No," Lenora said, "I don't think you should think that."

After a moment's thought, Hugh said he agreed with her.

BACK IN THE CLASSROOM

By the beginning of the fall term, Hugh was eager and ready for his classes. Each term brought new students into his classes, small multitudes of young people from different backgrounds, with comparable differences in abilities and expectations.

Grateful for the improvement in Lenora's condition, Hugh threw himself into his classwork with undiminished enthusiasm and vigor. When his students failed to understand why grammar and syntax and correct spelling were relevant to writing well, he resorted to all the various explanations he'd accumulated through the years: patient elucidation, hilarious samples of ruptured prose, scornful contempt for the intellectual laziness of those who presumed to write a poem or story without first learning how to write a correct sentence...all of these presented with what he knew could sometimes be a genuine theatrical eloquence, bedazzling students who often had little idea of what he was really saying.

Moonless Place

By now, he had once again made friends with his voice, and felt no compunction in calling upon it to beguile and infatuate as the occasion demanded. The desire he'd felt as a young man to write poems and stories seemed more remote to him with each year; there was something so pleasant about teaching the young what he knew, without feeling required to bolster his authority by citing "publishing credits" or referring to this or that book of his that had been well or poorly reviewed.

Once Lenora had told him that for a rational and essentially amiable man, he must have had a wonderfully strong ego to keep his life in focus and take so much enjoyment from it. He agreed with her, so far as seemed proper, but pointed out that teaching is itself a powerful stimulus for egotism, and should prove enough for people who had not been lured away from the true source of happiness by media superstitions.

And while he never forgot Elena Kolb, during the next few years he found himself thinking of her less and less often. And the poor dead girl's visitations in his memory were very brief—a luminous, pale image of an intense girl plotted against small, symmetrical handwriting in a journal. How strangely heroic she had been; how inhumanly disciplined.

And he had been privileged by having her listen to him talk, even in those last days when her suicide was growing in her mind, a dark building growing larger as it is approached in a car. How utterly inscrutable she was...if, as Lenora reminded him, what her mother had said was true. But if it wasn't? What a horror there was in that, altogether different from the courageous act of a doomed girl who chose not to wait for some bodily process to come to an end.

But he was old enough to accept a limited understanding of something that could never, in the nature of things, be entirely understood. And he often thought that even though the poor dead girl had possessed little if any talent for writing poetry, her life itself must have shimmered with something like poetic meaning...and now, in the dimming aftermath of her short, passionate, lonely and ignorant existence, she was fading into the sort of distance necessary for anything beautiful.

PROF. DEVLIN'S LAST LECTURE FOR HIS GOTHIC LITERATURE COURSE

Early this term I lectured on the word "Gothic," giving something of its origin and shifts in meaning. In it I pointed out how its architectural heritage was essential to understanding what we mean by the Gothic experience. I argued that

Moonless Place

ghosts, those most Gothic of creatures, can be said to exist only in some other room, whether that room be a literal, physical room, or metaphorically one of the divisions of past time. Ghosts are, in short, creatures of distance, and like most conceivable distances, they can be evoked only by language. Therefore, as I argued, Gothic narratives are intensely and explicitly linguistic in ways that other narratives are not.

In that lecture I also gave great emphasis to the fact that the rooms I was speaking of were not confined to those of the literal sort. They were not confined to the physical world, for people are sometimes trapped in far more fearful dungeons than those of iron and stone. Here, as in so many phenomena relating to the crepuscular world, Emily Dickinson's subtle testimony is worth attending:

> One need not be a chamber to be haunted.
> One need not be a house;
> The brain has corridors surpassing
> Material place.
>
> Far safer, of a midnight meeting
> External ghost,
> Than an interior confronting
> That whiter host.
>
> Far safer through an abbey gallop,
> The stones achase,
> Than moonless, one's own self encounter
> In lonesome place.
>
> Ourself, behind ourself concealed,
> Should startle most;
> Assassin hid in our apartment,
> Be horror's least.
>
> The prudent carries a revolver,
> He bolts the door,
> O'erlooking a superior spectre
> More near.

I call your attention to the grammatical skewing in the last line, in which the

Moonless Place

penultimate word carries the closed rhyme of "door," while "near" sustains the slant rhyme, ending the poem. But it is not the prosodic finesse that should occupy us here; it is the psychological character of Gothic horror—which is to say, its interiority. Therefore, now, in this last lecture of the term, I would like to elaborate upon and emphasize that idea.

In my previous lecture, I referred to Halloween as our Gothic holiday. As such, it naturally requires a Gothic structure, demonstrated by the fact that every October local chambers of commerce throughout the land seek out some old building to decorate and label a "haunted house" in order that small boys and girls can come there and be properly but comfortably and tastefully terrified. The fact that most of these attempts are so pathetically inadequate that even the youngest children are undeceived, let alone frightened, is irrelevant. As with unwanted gifts, it is the thought that counts...only in this case, it is the ritual.

And yet, the ritual is itself a mere shell of meaning. Because, as Emily Dickinson's poem argues, Gothic structures are not literally, and in the last analysis, places we go to, but inner presences waiting to be evoked. We can project our Gothic fears upon even unlikely things, converting them into some version of the crumbling mansion or decaying castle; but like all projections, these are intricately coded and they come from within. You may remember that in my previous lecture, I mentioned how in the classic horror film, PSYCHO, a motel— the most prosaic of structures—was gothicized.

If something as prosaic as a motel can be so eerily transformed, virtually anything can—providing, I repeat, it has two or more rooms. Since delivering my first lecture on the word "Gothic" I have had occasion to think about this aspect of the Gothic experience, and I want to explore it for certain deeper implications. Let us think of all enclosures as possessing Gothic possibilities. First, of course, let us think of the room we meet in, the room we are in at this moment. Think of this as one room among the many on campus; think of the campus as a Gothic entity, a veritable castle consisting of hundreds and hundreds of rooms scattered in the various buildings. As a concession to that literal mindedness basic to our sanity, I call your attention to the explicitly neo-gothic design of Steiger Hall and Clendennin Hall, lofty and vertical old buildings with all the arabesques conceivable to a Victorian mind, as cranky as the designs on leaves printed from the Kelmscott Press.

The vividness of this Gothic association is intensified when we think of all the various bureaucracies that constitute our university, each one a microcosm of sorts, symbolically charged, replete with information and the magic of expertise. Think simply of the electronic networks that both connect and separate our

Moonless Place

various departments and offices. Although these were all devised by human ingenuity, and we control and manipulate them for our own convenience and advantage, they have by the process of hypostatization become things in themselves. Not only that, they are all solidly rooted in one of the enduring and fundamental mysteries of our existence, electricity.

I am aware of how odd and even ludicrous it must seem to rhapsodize over electricity as some sort of mystical power, but that is only because it is so familiar a presence, one that so permeates our lives that we hardly know how to step back from it in order to see it for what it really is. We take it for granted, and it is hard to distance ourselves in order to understand how utterly ineffable this elemental force is. It is a force that we are able to manipulate without understanding, constituting a pattern of taboo that is implicit in virtually all science fiction. Moreover, its very indifference to the cultural colorations of our dreams and moods seems to remove it utterly beyond the reach of myth.

Furthermore, when we contemplate the campus buildings at night with their windows blazing with light, indicative of classes gathered to study such diverse and highly defined subjects as paleobotany, restoration drama, business ethics, and macro-economics...contemplating all this, we do not feel a Gothic presence. Not even the darkness of night—the essential Gothic element—can establish a kinship between this solid presence and those gloomy castles of institutionalized imagination. Not even that darkness compounded with that inner darkness we carry within us is enough to achieve such magical transformation. These compounded darknesses are not sufficient to evoke that "power of blackness" that Melville referred to in his review of Hawthorne's MOSSES FROM AN OLD MANSE.

None of these is sufficient except...except in the passing of time. When time is added, all things turn ghostly. Time is the essential element of change. Those archetypal stories that celebrate the theme of metamorphosis show time so concentrated that change occurs within the span of the story, altering an event or person radically from some previous state. And, as I argued in my first lecture on the word "Gothic," it is in the purviews and distances of time that both mystery and the symbol operate, paradoxically evoking essentially linguistic, hence human, perspectives.

What I am saying is, that as the familiar world where you find yourself during your college years—the university, the campus, this very room at this very moment...as this manifest world fades from the present moment and is increasingly translated into loss or memory, it will be transformed into a quite different sort of reality. As your friends and fellow students and even professors drift

Moonless Place

silently away from the present instant into the past, they will naturally and inevitably become more and more vague, nebulous, ghostly. Thus it is that all that is tangible insists upon becoming its very opposite in the slow ontological dance of enantiodromia—a dance which we are compelled to join simply by being alive.

But just as we all experience the things of the immediate present differently, so do we remember differently. It is, in fact, the interaction of our different memories with the present moment that renders the present moment unique to each of us. But beyond that—afterwards—we remember differently and to different degrees. While it may be argued that all of us are constrained to live inside our heads, some of us live there more vividly, more compellingly—I am tempted to say, more defiantly —than others.

And among these are a very small minority who experience time so richly, so differently, from the rest of us that it is as if distance itself is somehow encoded in their way of perceiving the world. Their sense of time is mythic, grand, ineffable. Their way of perceiving it is somewhat in the mode of fairy tales, whose formulaic openings are "once upon a time," and are therefore openings into what is tantamount to another ontological realm, one that is another sort of time, so different from the flux of our moments that it must be thought of as out of time.

I am aware of how vaporous and notion-riddled all this must seem to many of you, and how vulnerable I must be to charges of romantic obfuscation. But I am doing the best I can with a way of seeing that is alien to our language, so that the challenge of translating it is virtually overwhelming. If I could define and describe it better, I assure you that I would. And you would have every right to demand clarity of me if I were trying to articulate something as tangible as, say, the theory of the gyrocompass, or the relationship between the prime rate and the retail price index. But I do not know how to translate this large and complex and essentially mystical phenomenon into the languages of centrifugal force or institutionalized credit.

The people I am thinking about are extremely rare. In a way, they might be considered geniuses; only they are geniuses whose gifts are not manifest as are those of great inventors or scientists or artists. The people I am thinking of are possessed of the sensibility and insight of artists, without their gifts of expression. How, then, can they be called artists? You are right; they are not artists at all, but their lives are illuminated by the very light that artists strive to achieve through their media. It might be said that their lives are poems, in spite of—or possibly because of—the fact that they themselves are incapable of writing poems.

I think of these people as *fascinated*, in the old sense of the word which is to say, bewitched, entranced. I think of them as being possessed by what is essentially a Gothic destiny, for they live in that dimension of the past that is timeless, and the haunted castles they are imprisoned in are those inner corridors "surpassing material place," that Emily Dickinson understood and tried to describe for us. Although I will risk mystifying you by admitting so much, I will confess that I have glimpsed those corridors . . . and it was the sight of them that turned me away from trying to "be a poet." In this regard I am fortunate, for there are some who have no choice in the matter; there is no place for them to turn away *to*, so that they are trapped forever, or at least for as long as they remain what they are.

As humans, we are fated to make choices constantly; and we pay a price for every choice we make, even those that are made in the murky, ill-lighted offices of the bureaucracy of selfhood—offices which are connected by dark corridors of hypothesis and surmise. Let me personify that very small minority I am speaking of as a young woman, a girl, who cannot awaken from her trance. But if this girl I am thinking of...if she has made a choice, it was made so far beneath her awareness that she cannot trace her path back to it. So she is caught in a web of self-fascination, unable to express the powerful vision she is trapped inside. She yearns to do so with an indescribable passion—which is to say, she yearns to write poetry; but she is helpless. Perhaps it is fortunate for the rest of us that we catch only occasional glimpses of this towering obsession she is possessed by, an obsession greater than the vital principle, greater than life itself.

At the heart of her obsession is time. For time is the distance implicit in every other dimension of the castle of self where she is held prisoner. She does not want to escape so much as she wants to trace a passageway into the matter-of-fact, outside world; but she knows that the only way she could do this is by means of language...and looking upon the walls and corridors around her, she realizes with dismay that she is mute.

I have not been there, but I have had rare, quick glimpses upon that majestic and terrifying edifice, and I have therefore fancied that I sense how it must be with her. How else could I even attempt what I am attempting today, in your presence, in this very lecture? And how can I make it effective for you, if not entirely clear...for the sad truth is, it is not entirely clear to myself. Perhaps I can suggest something of its reality by referring to a parable I wrote when I was a very young man...before I decided that if becoming a poet required so profound and abiding a recognition, I would not choose to bother. I will warn you that this parable I wrote is sentimental, melodramatic and naive. But it exists, and it exists as an expression of what I once was. Therefore, given the awesomely ineffable character of the subject as I saw it then and still see it, its failure will perhaps not

Moonless Place

seem to be so spectacularly ridiculous.

In this parable, a poet stands weeping in the midst of a crowded market place. Seeing him, a friend comes up and asks why he's weeping. The poet answers, "Because of all these people. Look at them and how frenzied and busy they are, bustling about and selling and buying and caught up in the excitement of the moment."

"So what?" his friend said. "Why should something like that make you weep?"

"Because a century from now, they'll all be dead and gone."

"But that's ridiculous," his friend laughed. "You won't be here to see it."

"What are you talking about?" the poet said. "I can see it now!"

In this little parable, as well as in most of what I have been saying, you will recognize other sorts of ghosts from the historical past. You will recognize the doomed figure beloved of the Romantics, first, then Tennyson and his fellow Victorians, and on and on into various traditions that extend even to the present time. Sentimentalized and melodramatic, this tradition has enriched our lives in various ways, including those unflattering occasions for laughter it has provided. Indeed, few things are sillier than such over-indulgence in the childish *frissons* of pop spookiness. You have seen many of the teratological spawn of this tradition in the cheap and sensationalized flicks that creep into our TV sets late at night (although, I can't help adding, seldom late enough.)

These productions, and the facile responses which they invite, are so silly that they stain not only the medium, but the tradition which they exploit in their search for cheap-thrills-for-bucks. But if we are thoughtful, we should not let the poison travel back to its source. There is a Latin proverb, *Corruptio optimi pessima*, which tells us that it is ironically the corruption of precisely the best things that become the worst. Here we see another version of *enantiodromia*, that profound inclination within things to evoke and/or become their opposites.

But the poetry I am speaking of needs further definition. Poetry is made of words, to be sure; but in itself it is not words at all. If I could be sure that you believed in the soul, I would say that the words are only the physical body of poetry, but out of touch with its essence. What I am arguing for is a sense of poetry that so far transcends the publication of individual poems as the publication transcends those initial tentations into form that occur at the beginning of the poem's process.

What I am saying is, I believe it is conceivable that the vision, the inspiration, of a failed poet might be as great as or even greater than the vision of the most celebrated. Note that I do not say that the vision of this failed poet is greater than the published poem; I say that it might be greater even than the impulse behind it. I believe that poetry is not only more than "publication," it is more than language. As I see it, the paradox is that it is perhaps more independent of language than rivers, cornfields, slime, pebbles or virtually anything we can think of. Poetry is the one act which endeavors to escape language completely, utilizing its great power for the purpose of its ultimate repudiation.

But here, in my present context, it would be irrelevant to bolster such an assertion with logic and develop that argument, for I want to describe for you what is essentially a mystical sensibility that is or unknowingly strives to be free of the constraints of language. The female poet I am thinking of—a poet who does not and cannot write poetry at all, but is suffused with what for a better word we will call its transcendent meaning…this girl or woman is trapped in her own aloofness from success. Trapped on Parnassus, she finds herself inhabiting the essence of poetry, removed from the means to get there, which is to say, without a language.

But what she herself cannot understand is that Parnassus is not a public place at all, for it is beyond language, and language is our essential public act. Uncomprehending, she knows only that she cannot trace the path that has led her to the summit, for it is more as if she had been simply dropped there, and not led at all. She could not believe that she inhabited the destination, for she had earned nothing. She couldn't write a minimally successful poem, let alone "get published."

But what can that matter, after all? Pause a moment and think of Keats having to "get his work published"! Obviously, in some way or other, he did have to face up to this problem, just as every other writer must face up to it; but what bathos there is in that thought to us, today. Or consider Emily Dickinson, who in her Gothic room may have sensed it, which might explain the fact that no more than a dozen poems were published in her lifetime. And consider that popular mystical assumption that all good literary poems and stories will eventually—somehow, somewhere—be published. How can anyone believe such a thing? How many *unpublished* works do we know about?

You will remember that something like this is at the heart of Yeats' poem, "To A Friend Whose Work Has Come To Nothing." "Be secret and take defeat," Yeats' persona says to the failed poet—surely to some extent echoing his own doubts regarding the process by which the words of poetry are made public, which is to say, "published"; then he ends his argument, intoning:

Bred to a harder thing

Moonless Place

> Than Triumph, turn away
> And like a laughing string
> Whereon mad fingers play
> Amid a place of stone,
> Be secret and exult,
> Because of all things known
> That is most difficult.

To which one can only answer: is there anything other than "the most difficult" that can truly and permanently interest a poet, or to which a poet can aspire?

One aspect of that "harder thing than triumph" Yeats spoke of is neglect, which is social; but I would like to think that its other dimension—its *farther* dimension, I'm tempted to say—extends into that realm of pure poetry I have been thinking of, a realm into whose presence language can lead us, but which is itself beyond language…a fact that partly explains its inaccessibility. Poetry exists to point toward something beyond itself, which is to say, it is rooted in and comes out of the primary mode of signification.

Being beyond language, though to some extent communicable by it, this truth is ineffable, mystical, ghostly. We can see it only dimly, from that farthest reach where language can escort us, to that place where, faced with so distant and alien a prospect, it necessarily becomes mute—mute in the way of all mystical perception as it passes the boundary of earthly and describable things.

Now, having striven so earnestly to communicate this difficult and speculative truth to you, I will step back a moment and confess that, while my description has necessarily been abstract, I have actually known the sort of person I have presented to you as only a theoretical entity. She is not theoretical to me, even though I have been forced to theorize in order to understand her. I am speaking of a student, a girl, who once sat in one of the chairs in this room. She had no gift for writing poems, but in reading her journal, I eventually began to see behind her words, inferring something of the great existential burden that had been laid upon her life.

But it would be inappropriate for me to talk about this girl. More than most, her inner life was private and intense; more than most, it was immured in a silence beyond speech, and it would be *tabu* for me to try to break through. More than most, I eventually understood, she was a maiden imprisoned in a tower of remoteness, beyond all the power of language—hers as well as mine—to express; and it was her final act to seal this truth from all that is public and social, leaving us here to contemplate her unknowing testimony with humility and wonder.

JACK MATTHEWS is a native of Columbus, Ohio, and was a founder and director of the Creative Writing Program at Ohio University in Athens, Ohio, where he is now a Distinguished Professor. His six successful novels and six short story collections have earned him national recognition as a voice from the Midwest. He is also a renowned author on the art of book collecting with his *Collecting Rare Books for Pleasure and Profit* (Putnam, 1977) and *Booking in the Heartland* (Johns Hopkins University Press, 1986).

His short stories have appeared in *The Best American Short Stories*, *Prize Stories: The O. Henry Awards*, and *Best Ohio Fiction* (Bottom Dog Press, 1987). They have been collected in *Bitter Knowledge* (Scribners, 1964), *Tales of the Ohio Land* (Ohio Historical Society, 1978), *Dubious Persuasions* (Johns Hopkins Univ. Press, 1981), *Crazy Women* (Johns Hopkins Univ. Press, 1985), *Ghostly Populations* (Johns Hopkins Univ. Press, 1986), *Dirty Tricks* (Johns Hopkins University Press, 1990) and *Storyhood As We Know It and Other Tales* (Johns Hopkins University Press, 1993).

Matthews' novels include *Hanger Stout, Awake* (Harcourt Brace, 1967), *Beyond the Bridge* (Harcourt Brace, 1970), *The Tale of Asa Bean* (Harcourt Brace, 1971), *The Charisma Campaigns* (Harcourt Brace, 1972), *Pictures of the Journey Back* (Harcourt Brace, 1973) and *Sassafras* (Houghton Mifflin, 1983).

Tim O'Brien has described Matthews' fiction in the *New York Times* as "Filled with the wry and wistful insights of middle age...Matthews is a master of prose conversation and deadpan charm." Eudora Welty adds that the stories are "Blessed with honesty, clarity, directness, proportion, and a lovely humor."

Matthews' writing is consistently praised for its sense of language, its native humor, and its philosophical insight. In 1988, he received the Sherwood Anderson Fiction Award.